Further to Fly

Further to Fly

Black Women and
the Politics of Empowerment

Sheila Radford-Hill

University of Minnesota Press

Minneapolis • London

The University of Minnesota Press gratefully acknowledges permission to reprint lyrics from *Further to Fly,* by Paul Simon. Copyright 1990 Paul Simon. Used by permission of the publisher, Paul Simon Music.

Published by the University of Minnesota Press
111 Third Avenue South, Suite 290
Minneapolis, MN 55401-2520
http://www.upress.umn.edu

Library of Congress Cataloging-in-Publication Data

Radford-Hill, Sheila, 1949–
    Further to fly : Black women and the politics of empowerment / Sheila
Radford-Hill.
        p.   cm.
    Includes bibliographical references and index.
    ISBN 0-8166-3474-2 (HC : alk. paper) — ISBN 0-8166-3475-0 (PB : alk.
paper)
    1. Afro-American women—Political activity.   2. Afro-American
women—Economic conditions.   3. Afro-American women—Social conditions.
4. Feminist theory—United States.   5. Feminism—United States.
I. Title.
E185.86.R26 2000
305.48'896073—dc21   00-009073

Printed in the United States of America on acid-free paper

The University of Minnesota is an equal-opportunity educator and employer.

11 10 09 08 07 06 05 04 03 02 01 00   10 9 8 7 6 5 4 3 2 1

There may come a time
When you'll be tired
As tired as a dream that wants to die
And further to fly
Further to fly
Further to fly
Further to fly.

Contents

Preface

I read Simone de Beauvoir's *The Second Sex* ([1953] 1974) in 1971. My friend Alix Mitchell lent me the book and insisted that I read it. Although the length of the book was forbidding and much of it was decidedly over my twenty-two-year-old head, I remember being struck by its cogent and unrelenting analysis of the second-class status of women. Much of de Beauvoir's theory connected with and seemed to explain many of my own experiences in the peace, civil rights, and black nationalist movements. Although I did not understand it all, the book definitely left me with a new lens through which to view the social order. The idea that gender consciousness could lead to a new understanding of the power relations in society and culture transformed my thinking. Although I could not have foreseen this in 1971, I have spent the last twenty-eight years thinking about the implications of gender consciousness for social change. During those years, feminist theory has significantly contributed to our knowledge of how the world is or should be organized. Its promise of gender liberation through collective struggle has not, however, been fully realized.

Like many of us, I was a 1970s political activist whose experience with the gender hierarchies of radical protest movements was up close and painful. My campus peace activities, for example, provided me with numerous occasions to see and experience the marginal status of women in radical politics. My participation in the black nationalist movement directly exposed me to the gender dilemmas resulting from the inherent contradictions of black power politics. Because the politics of the liberation movements of the 1960s failed to include any substantive discussion of gender issues, some of us thought that feminist writing about sexual politics could in some way be applied to our situation. In those days, there was contentious interest in whether feminism offered an intellectual framework that could engender social change. I remember many and occasionally heated conversations about the utility of feminism both as a framework for challenging black women's positions in political movements and as a strategy for improving the social condition of black people.

After de Beauvoir, I continued to read feminist classics, such as Betty Friedan's *The Feminine Mystique,* Germaine Greer's *The Female Eunuch,* Shulamith Firestone's *The Dialectic of Sex,* and Kate Millett's *Sexual Politics.* I also became actively involved in a few women's issues, but after several years of organizing, protesting, and consciousness-raising, I was more than a little put off by the hysteria of early feminist bravado and much more than a little tired of the constant need to educate white women about their own racism. The more I learned about feminist politics, the more skeptical I became about the validity of a social movement based solely on gender. I acknowledged the need for struggle against male domination, but, like most black women, I took the position that racism was still the most dominant aspect of black experience. This position was buttressed by direct exposure to white feminist racism. Through this exposure, I began to understand that white feminists' fixation on patriarchal dominance masked their culpability for black women's oppression and for their own.

Although feminist politics was disappointing almost from its inception, feminist theorizing seemed more promising. The early feminist theorists and early black feminist writers and activists explored the social reality that I was experiencing and extended a vision of women and their relationship to the social order that was far more compelling than the vision provided by feminist politics or by nationalist-inspired black politics.

Throughout much of the 1970s, I was an active participant and skeptical observer. Black women spent significant energy resisting the reactionary roles envisioned for them by the radical left. For example, black women were often infuriated by the misogyny of the civil rights and black nationalist movements. They were marginalized and dismissed by the peace movement, and they were annoyed by the self-indulgent politics of the sisterhood. Although I enjoyed and loved many of the men in the so-called revolutionary vanguard—most metaphorically and a few physically—I knew instinctively that the political practice of these movements was disingenuous and contradictory.

In contrast to the political madness of radicals in search of liberation, feminist theorizing represented a serious attempt to envision alternatives to male hegemony in what I thought was the time between the defeated old order and the emerging new one. For this reason, I was especially renewed by the black feminist analysis of social reality. Like countless other black women, I read almost everything I could about black women and feminism. I soaked up the works of Toni Cade Bambara, Mari Evans, Maya Angelou, Sonia Sanchez, Carolyn Rodgers, Angela Davis, Alice Walker, and many other black poets and creative writers. At its best, black feminist theorizing was so irreverent in its dismissal of theories on the fundamental nature of society and so insightful in its efforts to describe and explain the impact of gender on social change that I slowly began to believe that a finely honed collective gender consciousness might empower black women's everyday struggles to change oppressive social conditions.

By the early 1980s, the creative and theoretical classics of black feminism had burst on the scene and turned mainstream feminism on its head. Black feminist writers such as Barbara Smith, Audre Lorde, and bell hooks demanded richer, more diverse forms of feminist theorizing. I reveled in black women's writing because it made my hurts, hopes, and dreams central to feminist discourse. As these writers struggled to shape a feminism that included women like me, their strident conceptualizations of the interaction of gender, race, and class helped explain how black women experienced and responded to multiple forms of social oppression.

As the 1980s progressed, however, black writers' depictions of black women became increasingly one-dimensional. Black feminists also participated in the presentation of Miss Jane Pittman–type, race-respectable portrayals of black women whose history had empowered them to overcome putrid conditions with dignity and pride. I began to be concerned about how these images were affecting ordinary black women, who were not responding to what I saw as a renewed need for active political struggle.

I became interested in looking at black women from an oppositional frame of reference. I contrasted the images of empowered black women with the real women I encountered in my professional and personal experience who were living their lives apart from any notion of empowerment. As one might expect, some of these women were poor, but many others were not. Social class was clearly not the defining characteristic of the self-determined black woman. With this in mind, I began to try to understand which black women, if any, were really empowered and under what conditions. In the process of resolving the contradiction between self-determined identity as a mark of empowerment and the existence of unempowered black women, I discovered that, compared to our historical traditions, black women's empowerment—which I defined as black women's agency expressed through social and political action—had actually declined.

Having discovered this loss of black women's empowerment, I was subsequently disappointed to learn that my discovery was very unpopular among both black and white women, in part because it coincided with the very moment in history when market forces and conservative politics were converging to make it appear as though black women's oppression was another relic of the general struggle for black people's liberation that America wanted to believe had already been won. In short, I made my discovery just as black women were being counted among the next generation of African Americans to reach the Promised Land.

Given the prevailing social and political climate, the go-go 1980s were a bad time to develop models to explain the decline of black women's empowerment. In the larger world, it was the beginning of Reagan optimism. It was also the beginning of the backlash against feminism, and all feminists were under attack. Furthermore, it was the beginning of the end of the sexual revolution, when feminist theory discovered postmodernism and even began to question the utility of concepts such as masculinity and femininity. It was a time when academic feminists declared independence from Marx and Freud while embracing Lacan and Foucault. It was, in short, a time when feminist theorizing was becoming accepted by the intellectual establishment, and because of its newly found respectability, it was beginning to fall in love with the sound of its own voice.

In a trajectory similar to that of other feminisms, as black feminism became more academic, its theoretical path led away from substantive analysis of the decline of black women's empowerment and the attendant decline of the black community. The virtual disappearance of feminist theorizing in local communities was especially problematic for blacks in poor and working-class neighborhoods.

Given the reactionary American cultural context of the 1970s and 1980s, black feminists were right to celebrate black women's contributions to American life. These celebrations did little, however, to address the unrelenting misogynist attacks that black women were experiencing both within and apart from the black community. Some feminists and black leaders—albeit for different reasons—denigrated black women's gender identity as culture bearers and community builders, whereas others pressed their demands for inclusion in a feminist movement struggling with its own racism. This structural dynamic created forms of black feminist theorizing that did not address, could not explain, did not predict, and could not account for the virulence of the attacks aimed at neutralizing the power of black women's agency.

As I continued to explore why and how this occurred, I found that the regression in black women's activism was intimately connected to the social disintegration and cultural malaise that exist among segments of the black community. In short, my research uncovered a crisis in black female identity that began more than thirty years ago and is still affecting large segments of the black population.

That feminist theory all but missed the way nationalist and feminist political practice contributed to the crisis intrigued me. What was the fatal flaw in feminist theory that left it incapable of conceptualizing race, gender, and power politics as they affected black women? In exploring this question, I began to realize that many academic women, especially those involved in women's studies, had vehemently complained about the disconnection between feminist theory and social practice. In the late 1970s, I dismissed these concerns as another one of those feminist squabbles that did not interest me. Later, I thought that the rift between academics and other feminist activists was a case of political differences over meaning in feminist theory. In the 1980s, however, as I reflected on the powerlessness of any feminism to explain what was happening to black women, I began to recognize the conflict between academic and activist feminists for what it really was. Activists blamed academic professionals for the disconnection between feminist theory and social practice because many academics, including black writers, were not seeking to engage people in the process of understanding their own social condition. Feminism, therefore, was no longer empowering women to change their lives and the conditions around them.

The debate between academics and activists was not a silly rift; it was a struggle for the soul of feminist thought and an indictment of the significance of feminist theory. Fewer than fifteen years after I first encountered it, feminist theorizing, with few exceptions, was no longer developing interrelated concepts and propositions that could be used to inform individual and collective decisions about how to act in/react to/survive one's environment. Far too many feminist analyses of social change left me needing the revolutionary rhythms of Sonia Sanchez and trying to figure out what feminist rhetoric had to do with the liberation of "nappyheaded blackgirls" like me.[1]

This book is part of an ongoing effort to understand how the lens of feminist theory and practice became so occluded that it lost its power to explain the decline of black women's empowerment. Academic feminists such as Joy James and T. Denean Sharpley-Whiting, among others, have acknowledged the shortcomings of postmodern feminism and the disconnection between academic feminism and activism. Few feminist writers, however, have identified the root cause of this dislocation in a manner that theoretically rebuilds the connections between feminist theorizing, social interaction, and cultural change.

The challenge of black feminism is to connect black theories of gender oppression with a renewed grassroots activism that resurrects black cultural power to rebuild black communities. As black feminists respond to this challenge, they will need to engage with, for, and on behalf of the struggles of black people. They will need to embrace black communities and to honestly confront antiquated sexual norms. They must challenge white institutions whose resistance to the full inclusion of their academic and professional interests robs black women academics of their agency and will. Only when black feminist theorizing rebuilds these vital connections can it become a catalyst for social change.

In the early years, black feminist theorizing was grounded in black life. Its soul, legitimacy, and significance emanated from the reality of black culture in all its myriad forms. From culinary art to architecture, from athletics to fine arts, from music to painting, from woodworking to literature, from textiles to textbooks, and from humor to horticulture, the creativity of black women was recognized as a source of cultural knowledge. To restore relevance, significance, and resonance to black feminist theorizing, feminists will need to position their theories much closer to the lived experiences of black women.

Further to Fly is a cultural critique of feminist theorizing, a critique that attempts to restore the power of feminist theorizing by reconnecting it to the social realities it should seek to explain. The book acknowledges the contributions and shortcomings of second-wave and postmodern feminism. In addition, it argues for more theorizing aimed at igniting a generation of women compelled to engage collectively in political and social action.

Books like this are never easy to write. First, it's never easy to find the time to read, think, write, rewrite, and rewrite again when you're a single parent, caregiver, wife, activist, humanist, educator, scholar, grandmother, and community leader. Second, it's never wise to reflect too much on your own past. Reflection is a killing revolution in this upwardly mobile, never-look-back, screw-you-too nation. But I persevere. I dedicate this book to those who have sustained me: Walter III, the remarkable one; Walter IV, my number one son; my dear friend Deborah Killingsworth, whose career in family medicine bears witness to determination; Erin, my sheer-energy niece; and the Mosleys for their ever faithful family support. I am especially grateful to Alix Mitchell, because without her friendship, patience, editorial wisdom, and, most of all, her hard work, this book would not exist. I also gratefully acknowledge my only daughter, Ericka Nayram. You are the hope for my tomorrows. May you soar. I am grateful to my friend Teresa de Lauretis and to the incomparable bell hooks, the feminists who personally encouraged me. Finally, I thank my Bethel Lutheran Church family, Bethel New Life, and all my friends whom I haven't seen in years—ever since I started writing this book.

Introduction

Theory provides the interpretive frame to make visible the daily and concrete social relations through which men and women create their worlds.

—**Heidi Gottfried, *Feminism and Social Change: Bridging Theory and Practice***

I

In basic terms, the purpose of feminist theorizing is to provide true and useful information about the meaning, significance, and impact of gender on human history. Feminist thought is the deliberative, polemic, speculative, and creative discourse from which feminist theory often emerges. Like all forms of theory, feminist theorizing posits an interrelated set of intellectual constructs that encompass interpretive frameworks. The purpose of these frameworks is to create knowledge that can be used to predict or explain how socially constructed sex roles and identities affect events, ideas, and relationships in the real world of lived experience (Pelto, 1970; Archer, 1988). Thus, feminist theory anticipates changing gender roles and creates explanatory frameworks so that the possibilities and consequences of these changes can be explored.

Because feminist theorizing deals with how gender influences aspects of human behavior, its theories adapt many forms of human thought and involve a variety of approaches to social issues (Gottfried, 1996, 9–12). Regardless of the form or approach that a particular strand of theorizing takes, its purpose is to catalyze action at specific moments in history. There are several basic questions that arise from the connection between feminist theorizing and social practice. For example, how does gender identity provide reliable information about a given social order? Or, put another way, can feminist theorizing meet the requirements of legitimate social theory? If so, what is significant about this, and if not, why not? Another set of questions relates to whether any strand of feminist theorizing is to be believed. Or, put another way, how can feminist practitioners know whether a specific form of theorizing constitutes a valid interpretation of women's lived experiences?

xv

Over the last thirty years, the connections between feminist thought and feminist theorizing, on the one hand, and empirical gender research and social practice, on the other hand, have become increasingly estranged. The reasons for this estrangement and its effect on black women's social activism are the subjects of this study. The book argues for feminist theorizing that aggressively connects to the realities of women's experiences, needs, aspirations, and responsibilities.

The term *authentic* is used to describe this type of feminist theorizing. Authentic feminism is not a new branch of feminist thought; rather, it is conceived as a desired characteristic of all feminist theorizing. Authentic feminism bases its research interests, methods, and strategies for the dissemination of its findings on the real needs of women as women themselves perceive them. These needs, in most instances, should be defined in connection to the values they represent. In this sense, authentic feminism is an applied feminism. As a methodology, authentic feminism uses participatory research methods to engage the discipline of scholarship on behalf of the interests and challenges of subordinate groups.

The use of the term *authentic* is not intended to recapitulate fractious feminist debates; rather, it is intended to affirm the feminist enterprise in all its diverse forms. Affirming long-upheld feminist values of political commitment, self-acceptance, individual transformation, and community is precisely what feminist theorizing needs to do to fulfill its destiny. In *to be real,* Rebecca Walker aptly describes this destiny as one that "challenges the status quo and finds common ground while honoring difference and developing the self-esteem and confidence it takes to theorize one's life" (1995, xxxv). To this I would add that authentic feminism affirms and reclaims communities as actual spaces or locations where groups of people build reservoirs of activism and love.

Authentic theorizing can avoid what T. Denean Sharpley-Whiting calls the pitfalls of feminist consciousness. Her discussion of these pitfalls in *Frantz Fanon: Conflicts and Feminisms* (1998) describes the need for a feminism characterized by its ability to organize liberationist projects among and with poor and working-class women.

Understanding the community-building process is an important characteristic of authentic feminist theorizing, because the values inherent in building community can be used to organize women across race and class (Naples, 1998). Incorporating coalition-based social and political action as part of building community involves the political self-interests of wide and diverse groups. Local community activism, when influenced by coalition-oriented women's leadership, can successfully initiate social change.

Authentic feminism supports local community activism and affirms the values represented by feminism both as an interpretive framework and as a historical tradition of women's intellectual and social action. Feminist research, therefore, can meet the requirements of legitimate social theory by using applied methods connected to local activism. Reestablishing the connection between feminist theory and social activism is vital to the resurgence of feminist theorizing as well as to the task of ensuring that all black communities are places of nurture and transcendence. Authentic feminist approaches to organizing, activism, and scholarship can result in larger numbers of black women who are involved in political activism and a narrowing of the current gaps between thought, theory, and action that still plague feminist theorizing.

Authentic feminism may renew black women's activism and reclaim their traditional roles as builders of community. The ability of feminism to restore black women's activism will be measured by the scope and impact of black women's involvement in political advocacy, local organizing, and initiatives to resist sexism and misogyny.

A clear explanation of the history and present limits of feminist theorizing illustrates the validity of the authentic feminist approach. For example, one could argue that second-wave feminism focused on the fundamental nature of gender and sexuality. Although this focus nurtured the many branches of feminist theory, it was too narrow and led to the fallacy of the unified female identity or the universal woman.

Strident opposition to the fallacies of essentialism refocused the political and social trajectory of feminist theorizing. In the process, feminism evolved from the discourse of patriarchy, domination, and women's oppression to the discourse of difference. Feminist theorizing shifted away from an analysis of the fundamental nature of gender identity to the various branches of feminist thought, such as liberal feminism, radical feminism, ecofeminism, black feminism, Marxist feminism, socialist feminism, lesbian feminism, and international feminism. Having to define and distinguish among feminisms entangled feminists in the sectarian politics of gender and identity. Much of the feminist thought from the mid-1980s through the early 1990s therefore labored over precise explanations about whose perspective a work represented (for example, lesbians, Jews, Latinas, or queers) or whose point of view it was intended to express. This preoccupation with the connection between political identity and particular strands of feminist theorizing is more reflective of feminism's self-absorption with the politics of its own identity than of the identity and empowerment dilemmas of women as individuals or as members of social groups. Thus, the political correctness of feminist theorizing imposed the tyranny of an acceptable identity on women struggling to define themselves. Consequently, the debates over forms of feminist practice combined with the politics of gender identity to produce an overemphasis on standpoint and perspective in feminist theorizing. In fact, how feminists defined themselves often became more important than how they needed to live as a consequence of their political choices. Over time, increasingly technical interpretations of gendered phenomena led to overspecialized postmodern discourses that, with few exceptions, failed to combat the emergence of neoconservatism, the glorification of politically correct stereotypes, or the predictable feminist backlash.[1]

Most women, especially young ones, simply became tired of gender conflict. They grew tired of political correctness, and they grew tried of obtuse, arcane, and often irrelevant debates about feminist identity. As a consequence, they abandoned feminism, because they saw little relevance between feminist debates and issues that needed to be confronted in their daily lives.

In the 1980s, feminist discourse became increasingly dominated by academic interests and dangerously separated from its activist roots. As a result, this discourse eviscerated itself by focusing on different aspects of its component parts rather than emphasizing the conceptual integrity of its thought and practice as a whole.

From the middle of the second wave to the present, feminist theorizing slowly neglected to create interpretive frameworks that included women's needs and values in its analysis of how gender relations affected the dominant social, political, and economic power relations. Over time the failure of feminism to provide guidance and direction to women in terms of their responsibilities to their families and their communities undermined its political utility and minimized its legitimacy.

These flaws in feminist theorizing have been discussed by many feminist writers (Clough, 1994; Walker, 1995), but the real impact of the disconnection between feminist theorizing and social practice on black women and on their communities has not been fully explored. In fact, despite major contributions to social theory, the history of feminist theorizing continues to fail black women, because feminist writers have not fully explained or provided reasonable alternatives to the devastating impact of black nationalism, white feminism, and the aftermath of these once raging debates on black women's gender consciousness. Thus, the shortcomings of modern feminisms have contributed to a decline in black women's empowerment. The precise nature of the decline, its impact, its aftermath, and its implications for feminist theorizing and black communities are the subjects of this book.

II

Further to Fly is a call to reinvigorate black women's political activism. The title of the book invokes the hope of future liberation and pays homage to the idea of flight as the quintessential metaphor of the black American experience. Flight symbolizes freedom from the bondage of slavery, release from the sickness of a relationship without love, and relief from the self-imposed shackles of anger and self-doubt. In slavery, flight was a marker of black resistance and therefore a constant torment to the slave master. Despite flogging, mutilation, and death, slaves struggled to escape the brutality of America's peculiar institution. Signs of flight were everywhere. Spirituals, folklore, work songs, quilt patterns, ring shouts—they were all calls to fly away or die trying. The metaphor of flight therefore captures black history and invokes the spirit of dreamers and inventors from the industrial age to the space age and beyond. The title of this book acknowledges our ancestors who brought us this far. It also affirms our understanding that there are miles to go before we sleep and that the promises made by, for, with, and because of us must be kept.

Chapter 1 begins with a broad exploration of the kind of feminism that would attract women who have abandoned feminism or have felt abandoned by it. Against the backdrop of a broad assessment of feminist theorizing, chapter 2 conceptualizes difference in a way that can illuminate the underlying dynamics of racial difference and social change. Because the connections between culture, community, and family, especially those involving the plight of children, will be the primary motivating force behind the rebirth of a black women's movement, chapter 3 explores the connections between black youth, culture, and community. Chapter 4 discusses the crisis of black womanhood, the cultural dynamics of black life, and the decline of black women's empowerment; and it illuminates the present state of black women's political culture. Chapter 5 argues that black feminists as well as other progressive elements of the American electorate need to confront the economic injustice that plagues the black community. The chapter discusses both the growing wealth and the entrenched poverty of low-income African Americans to demonstrate broad problems with U.S. economic policy. Chapter 6 reviews Michele Wallace's "Variations on Negation and the Heresy of Black Feminist Creativity" to explore how issues regarding black feminist creativity are often inappropriately framed. Chapter 7 is a cultural commentary that clarifies how feminists could, if they exercised the proper leadership, redefine major social and intellectual currents in contemporary America. Chapter 8 summarizes the main points of the book as part of a commentary on the Million Woman March, the long-awaited sequel to the Million Man March that took place on October 16, 1995. The Million Woman March attracted an estimated 600,000 to 1 million women to Philadelphia, Pennsylvania, on October 25, 1997.

III

This study was conceived as a forum for committed feminists and other women to begin discussing how to uphold the values peculiar to empowered people and communities. This book, therefore, invites people to think, speak, write, and talk about the revival of real feminist theorizing in ways that engender a spirit of community.

It is important to stress that for black women, rebuilding communities all across America means reclaiming the past, not repeating it. The traditional gender roles of black women have always revolved around building black communities. Black women have traditionally been culture bearers and community builders. In these roles, black women have strengthened black cultural resistance to the devastating impact of racism in its myriad forms. Historically, these roles were often unheralded and, in many cases, unappreciated.

Acting as reservoirs of the community's public morality and racial dignity did not always endear black women to those over whom they maintained a watchful eye. It is critical to note, however, that whereas historically these roles were criticized and sometimes taken for granted, after 1965 they were openly and publicly attacked. Of course, attacks against the intelligence and humanity of black women are nothing new (hooks, 1981; Giddings, 1984; Collins, 1991). Yet this particular period of attack precipitated a crisis in the role identities of black women that was unprecedented in its magnitude, relentless in its intensity, and far-reaching in its impact. This crisis continues to undermine the belief that black women can collectively sustain an active political culture that benefits them as well as their families and communities. It is the aftermath of a broad societal attack on the traditional gender roles that set the standard for black womanhood, an attack initiated by the liberal political and social ideologies of the Great Society that was supported by many black men and by large segments of the black community (James, 1996). The crisis was launched by a combination of research, political ideology, economic policy, media imaging, feminist activism, black nationalist rhetoric, and the influence of black community leaders.

In the 1960s, the politics of the civil rights and other movements shaped black women's social expectations. In their early years, these movements were defined by struggle, and gender was not allowed to become a significant issue. As the movements progressed, however, gender became not only a major issue but a flash point. The changes in gender and role expectations were swift and immediate. Consequently, black women of the baby-boom generation were not prepared to have their gender identities so intensely scrutinized. The wholesale rejection of black women's egalitarian approach to social change led to a rupture in black women's role identities. This rupture immobilized political consciousness, glorified political correctness, and led to widespread abandonment of traditional black female gender roles. Culture bearing and community building were devalued as oppressive to black women, matriarchal, or counterrevolutionary. Black women were forced to step away from their traditional roles without guidance, direction, or support. In the process, black women reduced their access to a cultural legacy of local activism. Ironically, this decline of empowerment and the abandonment of activism occurred precisely at the moment in history when community building and culture bearing were most needed to withstand the sweeping social and economic changes associated with the end of movement politics and the rise of social dysfunction, especially in low-income black communities (Wilson, 1987).

Paradoxically, despite a growing interest in the writings of black women and despite many noteworthy black feminist contributions to social and critical race theory, black feminist theorizing neither predicted nor explained the rupture of identity that I call the crisis of black womanhood. The explanation for this curious failure of black feminist theorizing lies in feminists' research perspectives as well as in the purposes and uses of their research. I raise the question, who was asleep at the switch when the crisis of black womanhood first started, not to figure out who is to blame but rather to show that these issues speak to whose reality is validated as knowledge. In other words, understanding the crisis of black womanhood leads directly to a critique of who is engaged in the production of feminist knowledge and for what purpose.

Although it is commonly known that the ruling elite use research to justify and to maintain their interests, it is also true that research can be used to provide an alternative to the status quo. Research can expand the basis and forms of analysis itself to include the interests of exploited sectors of the society (Freire, 1985). Most branches of feminism have been committed to linking research and action for the purpose of empowering previously oppressed groups to make fundamental transformations in society. Therefore, it is especially troubling that feminism has not always permitted black women to change the processes and forms of feminist knowledge in ways that benefit their culture and their communities.

IV

The call for black women to reclaim their standards of black womanhood acknowledges that the process of reclaiming traditional gender roles is not problem-free. Community, empowerment, culture bearing, and community building are fraught with conflicts and contradictions. As black women accept these responsibilities and adapt their gender roles to meet present circumstances, they will strengthen black communities and institutions. The process of reclaiming traditions of black womanhood can also revive authenticity in feminist theorizing. As black women creatively engage in changing their social condition, feminist theorizing and research can document the process of how women begin to define their social and political agendas in ways that are consistent with their needs, aspirations, and responsibilities.

This call for reclamation and reconciliation should not be mistaken as a simplistic plea for the return of the superwoman. This is not a call to embrace an unrealistic and unreachable movement identity. It is not a call to perpetuate a historical revisionism that requires all black women to be pillars of the community. Instead, this call to activism acknowledges, affirms, and uplifts our communities as powerful forces for social change. This call acknowledges that all can participate. It does not require black women to leap tall buildings in a single bound. There is no need to be what our mothers wanted or were. There is no need to justify our choices before the ceaseless scrutiny of our children. The idea is for black women to embrace each other in pursuit of the historical values inherent in black womanhood. Come as you are and do your part. All you need is an indignant heart, an insurgent spirit, and a willingness to act (Denby, 1989).

A commitment to authentic black feminist theorizing will result in strong, honest, and healing analyses of the black community. Black feminist research connects to feminist authenticity not by advocating one feminism but by exploring how ordinary black women understand their social condition and by working with and through them to engender their will and agency as a force for social change. The form and substance of feminist theory can be changed only by returning to the original purpose of that theory—to produce knowledge that helps change the world.

V

Feminist theorizing combines both science and art; it is grounded in the natural wonder of human behavior as well as in the many sorts of realities that behavior represents. The theorizing connects to phenomenal reality through empirical research. It is time for feminist theory and research to connect empirically, analytically, polemically, and aesthetically to the wonder of black women's experiences.

In the past, feminist research has consciously used multiple approaches to create understandings of the inequitable societal conditions faced by women and to uncover the legacy of activist resistance against human cruelty and injustice. Only the theorist who is skilled in loving observation, devoted to the painstaking gathering of evidence, and willing to shape the interpretive process to the demands of the enterprise will become privy to black women's gender secrets. Unlocking the secrets behind the needs, aspirations, and responsibilities of black women will reveal the values they feel are worth protecting. Understanding the connections and contradictions between these values will require patient observation and innovative theorizing. For black women, the creative use of gender consciousness conceptualizes seemingly disparate elements of black culture and community life as part of a whole.

Weaving together theoretical insights using disparate sources of experience and felt needs challenges the process of how feminist knowledge is produced, who produces it, and why. Sustaining this challenge is fundamental to a reawakening of black women's political activism. Black feminist theorizing is called to rediscover the salient connections among black women. Rebuilding these connections requires interpretive frameworks that restore black women's belief in collective action as a valid way to satisfy their needs and to fulfill their aspirations. If feminism is to play any role in this resurgence, the relationship between black women and feminism must be revisited so that feminism can be truly inclusive of difference. If feminist theory hopes to meet the requirements of social theory, it must both explain and predict how larger social structures will affect black women from the perspective of their needs, aspirations, and responsibilities. Revitalizing black women's political culture therefore requires forms of feminist theorizing that support the quest for social justice. Feminist theorizing should seek to understand the meaning and significance of social conditions while informing the movement and direction of social action.

This book argues for a new focus and direction for feminist theorizing. This new focus returns to the humanistic roots and activist orientation of feminist thought and reaffirms feminism's historical connection to personal freedom through collective struggle. A move to authentic feminism should lead men and women to radically different ways of conceptualizing masculinity and femininity and to fundamentally different reasons for doing so.

The best and most useful social theories explain, predict, and develop conceptual tools that explore the meaning and significance of social conditions while influencing the course of political action. This book is one small step toward these important goals.

1. Toward an Authentic Feminism

Sexual differentiation is already writ large in political theory in a manner that has so far served men. The solution is not to eliminate all such references (become gender neutral) but to recast the story with both sexes on stage.

—**Anne Phillips, "Universalist Pretensions in Political Thought"**

I

This book argues several basic positions, one of which is that feminist theorizing should become more authentic. Authentic feminism is rooted in the historical and present-day struggles for women's empowerment and self-determination. The concept of authentic feminism affirms the core values of feminist thought. These values include respect for all forms of women's creativity, an affirmation of diversity and difference, and a commitment to personal growth and political action. If feminism is to survive in the twenty-first century, its greatest challenge is to reclaim its core values and to restore its activist roots. Feminist authenticity depends on the capacity of feminist theory to construct new paradigms that place its fundamental values at the center of both discourse and social activism. The term *authentic feminism* therefore incorporates a characteristic of feminist theorizing that moves beyond marginal inclusion to the active engagement of black women at the center of feminist praxis.

Postmodernists and feminist intellectuals disavow the term *authentic.* To many feminists, the word *authentic* indicates a retreat from the feminisms of difference. No black feminist, however, would be remotely associated with a return to the time when feminism arrogantly erased its racism, classism, and sexism by wrapping itself in the mantle of common oppression and other forms of essentialism that silenced women of color. Any return to victim solidarity and to universalizing notions of feminism is dangerous and must be resisted. There is, however, no objective reason why *authentic* cannot be redefined and stripped of its incendiary baggage. In my view, authentic feminism insists on the primacy of liberation struggles. Its values are authenticated by women whose daily lives

1

challenge antiquated sexual norms and all forms of injustice based on gender, race, or class. These humanist values emerge neither from the essential nature of women nor from universal values that exist independent of human agency. Rather, authentic feminism represents a fundamental commitment to factoring gender, both as a social construct and as a corporeal reality, into the creation of human thought, the interpretation of human history, and the struggle for social justice (Barrett and Phillips, 1992, 1–9).

Authentic feminism draws its multiple languages and diverse expressions from the political logic of gender liberation as its various forms evolve in response to particular systems of oppression. When feminism returns to this humanist tradition of political activism, it will produce more authentic feminist paradigms. New feminist paradigms are needed to promote richer constructions of human sexuality, to engage stronger understandings of economic realities, to build more strategic coalitions, and to create deeper analyses of the way gender is socially constructed (Barrett and Phillips, 1992). As feminists create these new paradigms based on theorizing, activism, imaginative works, and other forms of creative expression, they must realize that feminist authenticity is ultimately contingent on how effectively women can teach themselves and others to integrate multiple theoretical and activist perspectives into significant and meaningful social change.

It has never been more important to clarify the purpose of feminism in the body politic than it is now. It is equally important to reach consensus on whose interests feminist theorizing ought to serve. Rapid economic, technological, and cultural change is creating both unprecedented challenges and historic opportunities for changes in the status of women. Because many critical social institutions seem unable to nurture human needs or to fulfill individual potential, women have a considerable stake in the search for new organizational and social arrangements. This stake creates an urgency for finding ways of living together that encompass genuine human values, meet real human needs, reconcile diverse social interests, and support the compassionate development and potential of human sexuality.

The unprecedented complexity of the social, political, cultural, and economic landscape is driving change in all forms of human thought. As knowledge itself is reconstituted, all feminisms must recognize that women are historically distinct, culturally different, economically diverse, and politically varied. Feminists who create more responsive paradigms will enhance the progressive and liberationist struggles waged by multiple groups on their own behalf.

Reclaiming feminist values moves feminist theorizing backward toward its activist roots and forward toward new theoretical insight and better ways of using a deeper knowledge of the world to change it. To this end, authentic feminism is a characteristic of feminism that connects theorizing to struggles for social change. Authenticity in this sense is neither a unitary political ideology nor a social orthodoxy; rather, it is part of the personal character of those who believe in gender as a source of human potential and who live their lives in ways that are consistent with that ideal. Authenticity is a consequence of living purposefully, of seeking to experience life fully by ending gender arrangements that hurt and maim us.

Of course, it remains to be seen whether feminist theorizing can become authentic in the sense that I am using the term. Although the feminist past is littered with racist thinking, cultural arrogance, false bravado, and superficial martyrdom, all forms of feminist theorizing have the inherent potential to connect gender consciousness to community in ways that affirm both individual human freedom and collective agency.

Within the context of principled, historically rooted, personally liberating, and community-focused paradigms, feminist theorizing can meet the greatest challenge of the twenty-first century, that of creating a world that refuses to replicate the repressive aspects of our gender-role relationships or the institutional discrimination that exists today. As both the content and context of feminist knowledge evolve, feminists can work toward a genuine unity that respects diversity and unites people around the ethics of social justice.

The goal of authentic feminist theory is to renew social activism. If feminism chooses authenticity, it will embrace many different strategies and approaches, along with diverse methodologies that encompass a range of intellectual disciplines, social concerns, and individual needs. In this way, feminist activism can improve the quality of daily life in all communities for women and their families by identifying and removing the underlying barriers to our collective well-being. These barriers must be identified and removed within the specific individual, cultural, economic, and environmental contexts where women live. Moreover, feminists should be ethically bound to enhance the life prospects for those women who are most disadvantaged.

II

The concerns of feminism have evolved over the past thirty years to include a range of issues related to gender equity as well as to the way gender both constitutes and is constituted by race, history, economics, culture, politics, and the human body itself (Gatens, 1992). Gender is an analytical tool used to focus on the social processes by which the meanings of biological difference are institutionalized within a given society. In recent years, some feminists have problematized gender by conflating that concept with those of women and sexuality (Oakley, 1997). Others have contested the use of the term *gender* (Sommers, 1994, 8–24). These arguments are meant to undermine the value of gender as a tool for understanding how societies mediate the continuum of masculine and feminine behavior. Contesting the concept of gender is often a political attack against feminism itself and should be taken in that light. Authentic feminism accepts both the utility and the pitfalls of gender. Gender is synonymous neither with sexuality nor with women. It is not inherently useful as a basis for political organization. That gender matters, however, is an underlying principle of all feminisms.

Feminisms use the concept of gender to theorize women both as serious objects of study and as serious subjects of social change. Authentic feminism acknowledges that there are differences in feminisms, some of which cannot be reconciled. Moreover, not all feminisms promote black women's activism. The work of authentic feminism involves understanding the complex political and cultural implications of lived experience in ways that neither conflate women's identities nor undermine the strategic solidarity essential to political action. Authentic feminism tries to explain and to predict ways in which particular cultures create and sustain gender-based social categorizations of "woman" over and against the aspirations of real women. It acknowledges that all women have a legitimate right to define their interests and to have those interests honestly debated as part of feminist practice. In the context of political action, authenticity demands a commitment to a search for common ground where all parties have an equal voice in the struggle to reconcile diverse interests in just ways. Authentic feminism demands the courage to embrace our values willingly and to live our convictions consciously.

III

Being black and feminist means accepting the social and cultural value of political activism. Having a black feminist identity goes beyond having the freedom to determine what I want for myself or the space to define who I am in connection with or in contrast to who someone else is. Having an authentic feminist identity means having the courage to stand up for important values in the world. I accept feminism, therefore, as part of my personal character and urge the creation of new paradigms to turn the feminist imperative in the direction of meaningful social change.

The social and political roots of authentic feminism emanate from a perspective on race and gender that stands in opposition to Euro-American cultural hegemony. Because white is deemed superior to black and men superior to women, cultivating a consciousness that resists the dominant culture's view of who and what I am has been critical to my survival.

Although a feminist political identity focuses my energy and my love, I fully understand that most black people in America consider feminism to be harmful to the task of black liberation. In fact, for many, feminism is an outmoded concept whose time has mercifully come and gone. Ordinary black women are particularly hostile to feminist thought. Their major criticism of the feminist movement is that it tokenized black women, ignored their contributions, and alienated them from black men and the black community. Some suggest that those who participated in feminist struggles were victims of a political boondoggle. For many women, feminism continues to be plagued by overreaching notions of women's identity, with no room for differences among women and no real concern for the impact of race and class on gender.

Given that my experiences with feminism have often been disappointing, I too have been tempted to accept these views. I realize, however, that allowing feminism to be defined solely by its weaknesses would suggest that women's oppression is a myth. It isn't. Moreover, a total disavowal of feminism would denigrate the struggle of those black feminists who infused nationalism with feminist consciousness and revolutionized the meaning of liberation. I owe too much to my history to bury feminism.

Today's feminisms confront the world in an ethical trajectory that connects me with hues and views of women's struggles around the planet. Moreover, black feminism positions me politically and defines the issues and concerns that give priority to my life and work. But in my view, feminism deserves to survive only if it can strengthen black women's efforts to change social circumstances that defy what we believe. The only way that feminism can step beyond token inclusion is to embrace its many colors and to wrap the core of its being around social and political action. In the struggle for justice, feminist discourse must seek to understand fully the multiple, disparate, and complex effects of gender on history and the importance of human values as expressed through culture and community. Restoring the power of gender, culture, and community is the unique contribution that black feminism can make. The term *black feminism* embodies this perspective and tells this story better than any other name (hooks, 1989; Collins, 1991).[1]

IV

What does feminist authenticity mean for black feminist theorizing? Within the pursuit of liberation, black feminism asserts the plurality of difference and is committed to affirming this diversity in ways that ultimately transform the status quo. Being a black woman allows but does not require one to cultivate a racial identity that affirms the African American tradition of cultural resistance. One needs to recognize, however, that being a black woman also means being caught in a web of multiple and synergistic oppressions. Thus, black feminists challenge unitary, xenophobic, and chauvinistic notions of women's oppression and human liberation. Their feminisms affirm black traditions and bring cultural knowledge to bear on the issues that affront black people and affect everyone. Because black feminism has been a countervailing force against the excesses of both liberal and conservative feminist thought, it has also challenged white feminists to come to terms with richer and broader paradigms of gender and sexuality than those they originally conceived. By asserting the inherent value of pluralism, black women helped feminists to see differences in womanhood as part of a rich tapestry that all women have an obligation to foster.

It is important to acknowledge black feminist contributions to feminist theory gratefully, but it is equally important to recognize that these times demand a reordering of black feminist priorities. Black feminists are being challenged to empower black female leadership at all levels in the struggle against race, class, and gender subjugation. Before they can actively sustain pluralistic coalitions with white women and other women of color, black women must first ignite the process of moving black people together in a strategic direction. Black women must recognize that their personal goals for economic security and legitimate life options are inextricably linked to their willingness to assume authority, responsibility, and stewardship in the communities where black people have traditionally lived. As women whose gender and sexuality have been principally defined within the context of the failures of European and American cultural hegemony, black feminists are central to the process of integrating the fragments of black political culture and of strengthening the community institutions that shape black life.

Authentic feminist practice calls for black feminists to formulate a vision of community as part of its core values. In this context, the black feminist vision embraces our traditional community-building values and is premised on what Patricia Hill Collins calls the ethic of caring and the ethic of personal responsibility (1991, 125). Black feminists cannot become cloistered or silent as black women endure circumstances that destroy their dignity and endanger their physical well-being. They cannot avoid organizing for political action within local communities. And they cannot avoid organizing to eliminate sexism, homophobia, and misogyny from black communities.

V

In the new millennium, black women must put the goal of building healthy black communities first. They can demonstrate their commitment to this goal in five ways. First, middle-class black women have to deepen their personal connections to black people in inner-city neighborhoods and isolated rural communities. There can be no real understanding of poor people's experiences and needs when class divisions lead to almost total separation or to an uncomfortable social proximity that is mediated either by the government or by academic institutions.

Second, middle-class, working-class, and poor black women need to accept the challenge of creating feminist consciousness in the black community. Black women need to step up their organizing to repudiate gender terrorism in the form of child abuse, domestic violence, hate crime, and criminal sexual assault. This means that black women have to put their minds, money, bodies, institutional resources, and political capital on the line. We need to work together to build coalitions that empower community people and that change public policy to make institutions more responsive to people's needs. A wide range of institutions benefit from the subjugation of black knowledge, the sexual exploitation of black women, and the incarceration of black men and women. The politics and policies behind these institutional arrangements need to be challenged and changed.

Third, black feminists should strive to heighten political consciousness among black people. The organizing and activism involved should empower black women to heal from past and present dysfunctional relationships and from the deep wounds between black men and women. Fourth, black women need to promote gender norms that nurture our children while strengthening our diverse forms of family life. Finally, black feminists should promote direct action that respects grassroots leadership, refuses to blame victims for their misery, and builds strategic alliances across race and class to improve black social and economic opportunity.

Meeting these challenges will require black feminists to place a new emphasis on struggle. For this reason, black women are required to reclaim their historical role in the black community. Resuming our role as mothers, culture bearers, and community builders can move poor black communities from the brink of destruction and enrich all our lives — wherever we live. Black feminist ethics places women's leadership in the service of effective social action. Authentic feminist theory informs specific strategies for local community action and broader political agendas that are sharpened and refined through the dynamics and synergies of grassroots social change.

VI

Any articulation of feminist values raises several issues that must be addressed. The first issue is that of living the values claimed by our discourse. Living our values requires commitment and discipline. Black women must continue to cultivate necessary habits of mind, including observation, oppositional analysis, action, reflection, and compassion. Another issue that must be confronted involves a question: Can white and black feminists use a value-based feminism to get beyond the history of exploitation and privilege that bitterly divides them? The answer is no, at least not entirely. Practical wisdom suggests, however, that if we can't be sisters in victim solidarity, maybe we can be partners in a focused political solidarity.

The survival of feminist theorizing will depend on women's capacity to take political action. Future political alliances will need to rely not only on goodwill but also on political interdependence and partnerships that advance mutual interests. In the past, feminists made the mistake of trying to decide, in the face of inevitable conflict, whose political solutions to social problems were more legitimate, based on who was more oppressed. Although this approach is extremely tempting for those of us who have endured generations of brutal repression, it uses dead-end logic that doesn't get us anywhere.

To avoid repeating such fatal mistakes, authentic feminism demands a commitment to women's leadership. As part of its authenticity, black feminist theorizing needs to build black women leaders consistently. This leadership needs to be fundamentally different from the failed charismatic, phallogenic, ethically corrupt, and discredited leadership created by American political culture. Black women can raise up and support leaders who are visionary, pragmatic, inclusive, and accountable. Embracing the challenge of building genuine black leadership allows black women to participate as equals in the process of reshaping social, cultural, and economic institutions to meet the demands of a socially just world.

Authentic feminism is a demand within feminist theory that encompasses a recommitment to humanist values and social activism. It incorporates the concerns of contemporary feminist practice and is committed to engaging the justice and diversity issues raised by black women and other women of color. Authenticity evolves from consciousness to theorizing, from theorizing to action, and from action to reflection.

The success of feminist theorizing is directly connected to the degree to which women consciously live their values and the extent to which they are prepared to intervene directly in the world around them. Energizing black feminist theorizing is an important step in building an authentic feminist tradition. An increasing number of feminist-activist scholars have successfully negotiated the challenge of linking their research agendas to the needs and goals of women activists. As their work chronicles women's activism, it reinvents feminism as well. Building black community requires activists to pay more attention to the wisdom and class perspectives of those involved in these struggles. If we accept our responsibility to shape this approach to feminist social action, authentic feminism can revive black women's political traditions.

2. Uses and Limits of Black Feminist Theory and the Decline of Black Women's Empowerment

NOW is dedicated to the proposition that women . . . must have the chance to develop their fullest human potential.

—National Organization for Women, statement of purpose, adopted at the organizing conference in Washington, D.C., October 29, 1966.

In the radical feminist view, the new feminism is not just the revival of a serious movement for social equality, it is the second wave of the most important revolution in history. Its aim: the overthrow of the oldest most rigid caste/class system in existence, the class system based on sex.

—Shulamith Firestone, *The Dialectic of Sex: The Case for Feminist Revolution*

This chapter discusses the relationship between second-wave feminism and the decline of black women's empowerment. In the context of a movement whose explicit goal was to raise women's consciousness and engender social change, black feminists made little progress in creating feminist theories that could mobilize black women on behalf of black culture and community. The insights of feminist intellectuals and the acceptance of black feminist thought in academia should not be allowed to obscure the fact that neither gender consciousness nor liberation politics addressed the political and cultural damage that the Great Society and its dismantling did to black male-female relationships and to the social fabric of black communities across America. Furthermore, feminists have been demonized by a backlash that holds feminist theory and politics responsible for the decline of American civil society, the loss of America's moral values, and the general lack of political participation and social activism that characterizes America in the information age. Although these charges are overblown and unfair, feminists should not ignore them. The times demand constructive responses to the criticism that feminist theorizing is failing to shape gender consciousness to fit the demands of a new century.

Although, in general, feminist paradigms are shifting in response to the changing realities of race and gender, it is time for black feminists to rethink the purpose of their theorizing so that the impact of gender on history remains accessible and relevant to new generations of black women. If it is true that theorizing makes an important contribution when it enhances our understanding of race as a gendered reality, then at least two questions arise: How can black feminists theorize the complex dynamics of gender difference? And how can race be usefully conceptualized as part of the dynamics of gender identity? This chapter explores these questions and offers a model for conceptualizing differences among women.

I

Feminist theory, irrespective of its political perspective, examines the forms, functions, and social processes of human sexuality and explores the dimensions of gender in a variety of contexts. Feminist analysis is meant to influence gender consciousness and to catalyze individual transformation and progressive social change. In other words, the main use of feminist theorizing is to promote women's empowerment. In the current political context, empowered individuals are self-determined but value difference, diversity, and community.

Empowerment is a term contested by feminists themselves. For example, Nira Yuval-Davis states unequivocally that "empowerment of the oppressed cannot by itself be the goal of feminist and other anti-oppression politics." She argues that empowerment politics "naturalizes social categories and groupings, denying shifting boundaries, internal power differences, and conflicts of interest" (1997, 97). Although I understand Yuval-Davis's concern, I am troubled by a logic that uses one aspect of empowerment to define the whole concept. The politics of empowerment is fraught with the contradictions imposed by differences in power, scarcity of resources, conflicts of interest, and shifting alliances. But true empowerment is not just political. Genuine empowerment is a process, not an event or an endgame. Its goal is to define individual and group self-interest in the broader context of social justice. True empowerment goes beyond the group's responsibility to protect its turf or to control decisions that affect its members.

When leaders are allowed to conflate empowerment and politics, the result is as Yuval-Davis suggests. However, if empowerment processes are widely institutionalized, different individuals and groups have meaningful access to the structures that exercise power and influence. Focusing on empowerment as the primary goal of feminist analysis therefore compels black women to reconceptualize feminist theories of racial difference and to affirm the direct connection between gender theorizing and social action.

Gender hierarchies subjugate the feminine and advance different values about the way the world ought to work. Because black women and other women of color experience gender difference as the denial of access to social, economic, and political power, their empowerment requires progressive social change. Thus, black feminist theorizing confronts women's subjugation as a perversion of a just social order.

Because racial differences are mediated through gender, culture, class, region, and personal experience, they compel black social theorists to visualize alternative uses of power, modes of production and exchange, labor, religious traditions, political systems, and personal identities, each in opposition to prevailing norms. Black women's activism therefore scrutinizes social processes and promotes alternative values as the bases for renegotiating gender roles and responsibilities. In this context, black feminism operates as an interpretive force between the cultural meanings of gender and the social uses of power.

II

In the second wave, black feminism evolved in response to exclusion from a social movement whose theoretical discourse held liberating potential. Current critiques of second-wave feminism focus on the limits of victim feminism and the downside of the liberal feminist push for gender equality. Feminist critics sometimes forget, however, that despite these shortcomings, the second wave privileged gender and valued women's community. The shortsightedness of faulty logic should not deter history from crediting the second wave for connecting women's political activism to humanist values and for its professed desire to create forms of community that valued women's experiences.

Alternative ways to conceptualize and use power were the hallmarks of second-wave feminist analysis. The social construction of gender, the personal nature of female oppression, the sociology of gender hierarchies, and the victimization inherent in social institutions were refined and distilled through an active network of feminist grassroots activities. These activities included political action, consciousness-raising, organizing to resist sexism, and advocating on behalf of issues affecting women, such as gender discrimination, women's health, and reproductive choice, to name a few. Although feminist alternatives to the problems of contemporary society were not as radical as second-wave feminists might have thought, their feminism managed to ignite a women-centered political activism that black feminists tried but failed to extend to the black community.

Despite its shortcomings, in its halcyon years second-wave feminism engaged women in social action, strengthened their commitment to women's personal growth and political liberation, extended their rights both as human and as sexual beings, and energized a core of creative theorists and intellectuals who created a rich body of systematic thought. These actions left women a legacy of how to lead politically conscious and otherwise empowered lives.

Yet the limits of second-wave theorizing outweighed its strengths. The theoretical insistence on sexism as the most fundamental of all oppressions and the inability to develop a framework for the affirmation of difference limited the impact and utility of feminist thought. The more that second-wave feminist theorizing portrayed women as social constructs defined solely by oppression, the more obscure the theoretical connection between being empowered and taking individual responsibility for sustaining community became. Feminism's insistence on the primacy of sexist oppression simply ignored the relationship between race, gender, and class while obscuring the race and class privilege of feminists themselves.

The notion of women's victimization subordinated all women to an essentially white, middle-class political agenda that arrogantly dismissed women's diverse values, needs, goals, allegiances, and aspirations. Feminist orthodoxy closed off ideas and insisted on allegiance to a string of politically correct behaviors (e.g., man hating, civil disobedience, and rabid sisterhood), each of which was required no matter how inconsistent these behaviors were for women with different experiences. As a result, feminism, in most of its political forms, became a string of repressive ideologies. Black feminists and other women of color began to argue for difference and diversity without ever being able to create a movement to realize the full implications of their demands. Instead, black feminist protests often simply absolved white feminists of the responsibility to engage deeply the complex issues surrounding race, ethnicity, and gender. It was simpler to tokenize black feminists or women of color by creating yet another category of feminist ideology.

Feminisms became so narrowly defined and so politically reactive that fierce battles for feminist hegemony became the norm, and legitimate charges of racism, anti-Semitism, and homophobia all but ended movement politics. Splintered and fragmented, the proliferation of feminisms and the demagoguery of most feminists dissuaded many women from going beyond the negative images that portrayed feminism as a short-lived movement involving privileged and self-absorbed suburban housewives who wanted to get jobs because they were bored at home. At the height of the backlash, most feminists became synonymous with women who, after fighting to gain access to the labor market, became bored at work and concerned about their "biological clocks" and were therefore exercising their self-absorbed right to go home and have babies because they were tired of "having it all" (Brown, 1982; Faludi, 1992). Feminism became an ideology that deserved to die.

In the final analysis, the second wave was too self-absorbed and too fractious to understand that women's power is neither an essential quality of the female sex nor a by-product of common oppression. As the fiery rhetoric and essentialist claims of the 1970s settled into the subdued and reflective feminism of the 1980s, this self-conscious feminism went in search of a more precise understanding of its questions, methods, and structures of inquiry.

In the 1990s, feminism became increasingly dominated by women in academia. As feminism gained intellectual legitimacy, feminists understandably became more concerned with their relationship to the intellectual establishment. The resulting emphasis on postmodern and situated knowledge employed a discourse designed in response to the competitive interests of intellectuals. Feminist discourse focused intensely on the relationship between identity and its representation, and lost its connection to women's empowerment.

During the ascendancy of postmodernism, feminists argued that its theoretically precise discourse was an antidote both to the alienation caused by feminist doctrine and to the epistemological lapses of the information age. As a whole, however, postmodern contributions to feminist theory miss the mark. They are not sufficiently connected to political activism and therefore do not benefit the masses of women for whom feminism was initially intended. Moreover, although poststructural theories demonstrate how cultural domination gives hegemonic power to one group's point of view, this is not the same as working with, for, and on behalf of oppressed, marginalized, or economically exploited people (Hartsock, 1996; Huntington, 1997).

The value of second-wave feminism was its struggle for voice and consciousness. In contrast to this activist orientation, postmodern feminisms emphasize specific social processes that define the experience of being a woman. These analyses explore the internal contradictions posed by human sexuality but are less interested in creating social and political systems that help women sustain self-determined gender identities. Postmodernism is richly descriptive but largely disconnected from communities that need leadership and direction. The use of exhaustive microanalysis is limited without the clear and present purpose of social transformation.

Similarly, although articulating stance and standpoint is fundamental to black feminism's acceptance as academic discourse, standpoint epistemology, or a theory of knowledge based on an individual's relationship to the broader society, is ultimately an insufficient conceptual framework for effective social change. One reason is that standpoint epistemologies do not sufficiently acknowledge the ability of those in power to create and enforce the dominant standpoint. Another reason is that the standpoints held by those not in power are not inherently legitimate or equally correct. Thus, any subordinate cultural system that competes within a cultural hegemony periodically needs to reorder its focus fundamentally to thwart co-optation or destruction by the dominant culture.

In postmodern discussions of the politics of empowerment, situated knowledge correctly envisions each unique standpoint coming together with others in search of larger truths. However, the hidden agendas and contradictions inherent in articulating and reconciling different truths necessitate more than the mere relinquishing of power by the dominant group. Empowering the unempowered is a war of resistance on multiple fronts, with enemies positioned simultaneously within and outside of the subjugated group.

Within the context of multiple oppressions and the stigma of racialized identities, black feminist theorizing confronts changing political, economic, and social contexts to analyze how issues of identity impede the formation of an empowered gender consciousness. Understanding these complexities is fundamental to conceptualizing diversity and difference as the dynamic social forces they really are.

Although difference has emerged as a critical concept in postmodernist feminisms, the unexamined questions surrounding its meaning, significance, and value allow the concept to disintegrate into a welter of relativism that mystifies feminists' very reasons for theoretical precision. To investigate and appreciate diversity is of strategic importance to feminist politics; therefore, a clear and honest understanding of how groups of women differ from each other is a necessary aspect of reasserting the power of ordinary women to claim the connections between them. A framework for understanding difference and diversity is necessary for "thinking through and empirically studying how differences among women are relationally constituted" (Liu, 1994, 574). A strategic framework that conceptualizes difference in this way allows theorists and researchers to understand how women's differences emerge and how they work in relation to each other. Such a framework specifies the individual and communal aspects of women's

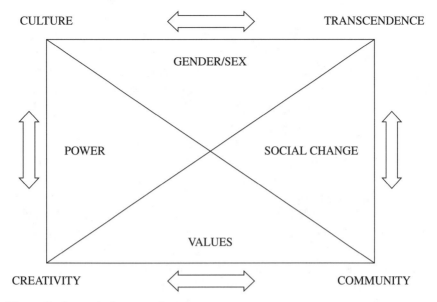

Figure 1. Strategic framework.

experiences that constitute difference, and emphasizes that these dimensions should be understood as parts of the whole.

The framework I propose contains four social arenas or domains: gender/sex, social change, power, and values. These four arenas allow differences to be understood socially and relationally. The parameters of the framework are aspects of the dynamic intersection of two axes of identity: culture and community, and creativity and transcendence. The individual aspect of women's identity revolves around their creativity and transcendence, both of which are used to construct social meanings from personal experiences. The communal aspects of identity revolve around culture and community. Community entails family and socialization rituals, including norms, myths, and traditions.

These two intersecting axes symbolize the social, cultural, and psychological dynamics around which women organize their needs, aspirations, and allegiances. A woman's relationship to her culture and community is one axis of her identity. How she operates her consciousness to transcend social, psychological, racial, class, or ethnic barriers and how she uses creativity in that process constitute the other.

Culture is usually defined as attitudes, group norms, values, and customs that are passed from generation to generation and recognized by a social group as part of its heritage. The proposed model conceptualizes culture in a more complex and more varied way than the usual definition implies. Cultural systems, in this context, are abstract and dynamic interactions that result in dominant ideas being held among specific groups of people at any given time. Within the model, culture is conceptualized in terms of its ideas, the structures that groups develop to maintain ideas favorable to their interests, the responses of other groups to these ideas, and the interplay between groups and ideas. As culture is a dynamic interaction between and among people and ideas, it is a mistake to assume that culture presents a set of totally consistent ideas or beliefs. Culture influences human behavior through ideas, but the mediating structures between ideas and people can enhance or impinge on cultural agency, that is, the capacity of culture to influence behavior.

Community is defined as a specific space, location, or grouping of individuals whose sharing in common is claimed by and valued as a significant aspect of an individual's identity. Feminists, among others, have argued that the notion of community is problematic, because most people belong to overlapping or in some cases multiple distinct communities with their attendant divided loyalties. Although people's sense of community may shift over time and across different groupings, the need for community remains even as those shifts occur.

Transcendence is defined as an individual's psychological and spiritual capacity to move beyond the material conditions of subjugation. Transcendence involves reflecting on the material conditions of one's existence in ways that address the meaning and purpose of one's life. From this aspect of the human psyche, people can connect their lived experiences with their perceptions of the broader meaning of existence.

Creativity is defined as the capacity for problem solving or innovation that transforms a particular cultural domain or significantly affects a field of endeavor (Gardner, 1993). Creativity also invokes the sense of triumph over subjugation that Alice Walker discusses in her essay "In Search of Our Mothers' Gardens." Walker writes:

> How was the creativity of the black woman kept alive, year after year and century after century, when for most of the years black people have been in America, it was a punishable crime for a black person to read or write? And the freedom to paint, to sculpt, to expand the mind with action did not exist.... Then you may begin to comprehend the lives of our "crazy," "Sainted" mothers and grandmothers. The agony of the lives of women who might have been Poets, Novelists,

Essayists, and Short-Story Writers (over a period of centuries), who died with their real gifts stifled within them. . . .

But this is not the end of the story, for all the young women — our mothers and grandmothers, *ourselves* — have not perished in the wilderness. And if we ask ourselves why, and search for and find the answer, we will know beyond all efforts to erase it from our minds, just exactly who, and of what, we black American women are. (1984, 234–35)

As there are significant generational, cultural, racial, ethnic, regional, and experiential differences among women, understanding the range of their responses to gender/sex, power, social change, and values engenders theorizing that explores how women envision themselves, their roles, their resources, and their abilities to alter prevailing social norms. Using a strategic framework, black feminists can conceptualize the interaction between identity formation and the demands of an empowered self. In this way, a strategic framework or model of women's differences can help sustain black women's social and political activism while clarifying the conditions under which broader coalitions can be formed. The use of a strategic model can also influence the task of energizing black activism and rebuilding black communities in decline.

Energizing black women's political culture requires that feminists influence the standards of black womanhood used in the process of black women's identity formation. One aspect of identity needs to reconcile an empowered self to culture and community. The other aspect involves increasing the individual's capacity to operate his or her own consciousness in ways that nurture transcendence and creativity.

The strategic framework shown here conceptualizes the dynamic relationships between gender/sex, power, social change, and values. In addition, the connections between community, creativity, transcendence, and culture are depicted as dynamic and interactive aspects of difference. As a model for understanding women's differences, the framework highlights how alternative political analyses are developed and nurtured over time.

As depicted within this framework, power is defined as the capacity to produce a desired result or outcome based on specific changes in individual or group behavior or on adherence to group norms. Power is predicated on an implicit or explicit social contract and is conveyed by authority, coercion, status or wealth, and tradition or leadership. Values are defined as beliefs about the need for a desired state of being or state of affairs. Values are predicated on principles that people deem important, that is, those that are worth articulation, reflection, and sacrifice. Gender denotes the role of human sexuality defined as the cultural meanings represented by the continuum of masculine and feminine difference. Sex is defined as biological difference but denotes how gender difference is expressed. Social change is characterized by the ability to alter power relations or the means by which power is conveyed. Social change encompasses differences in social relations that evolve or are coerced in response to cultural, economic, political, technological, social, or ecological processes within and across specific historic contexts.

In opposition to linear approaches to social change, the proposed framework involves understanding how gender and sexuality interact to maintain or to alter the traditional social order. Thus, the strategic framework can be used to articulate the significant cultural, racial, and ethnic differences that influence how women view their roles, resources, and abilities to alter prevailing social norms.

In the relational model of difference, race is viewed not as a separate domain but as a way of constructing human experience that operates across all experiential domains. Critical race theory informs the concept of race and its connections to black liberation envisioned by the model. One fundamental concern for critical race theory is the stigma attached to being black. Lewis Gordon, for example, describes what he calls "the symbolic order of Western Civilization whose place for the black has been fundamentally negative as far back as the Middle Ages and antiquity" (1997, 3).[1] Gordon, Lucius T. Outlaw (1990), and Patricia Huntington (1997), among others, contend that as long as whiteness is a structure of privilege, blackness will be an important psychological and social location for the development of political consciousness.

Although this view is consistent with the writings of black feminists, some theorists resist the stigmatization of "the black" by rejecting race-based or racialized identities. For example, Naomi Zack asserts that race has no genetic or biological base. Rather, it is "a complex of myths and social fictions that form a powerful cultural identity." Zack argues that race should be "reread" as the result of "a web of lies told about oppressed people by their oppressors to justify their oppression." For Zack, blacks who accept or cultivate racialized identities endorse the oppressors' lies (Zack, 1997, 100).

From a different perspective, K. Anthony Appiah also argues against race-based notions of identity. He asserts that racial groups in the United States do not share common beliefs and rejects the notion that race is connected to a separate and unique cultural identity. Thus, race is not an appropriate vehicle for organizing aspects of identity. Appiah argues that if blacks want their freedom from identities ascribed to them because of race, they will have to move beyond current racial identities (Appiah and Gutmann, 1996, 87–93).[2]

The merits of these and other positions regarding race deserve continuing and extensive debate, but the most important aspect of race for this discussion is not how or whether race matters. Rather, it is the fact that race is always present and available to be used in the construction of one's identity or in efforts to construct meaning out of one's lived experience. A refined and disciplined understanding of the history, the limitations, and the possibilities of race therefore adds urgency and power to our understanding of difference. Moreover, an understanding of racial injustice can strengthen the personal commitment of human beings to freedom and justice for the world's subjugated people (Fox-Genovese, 1991; Appiah and Gutmann, 1996).

In this context, racism is not simply prejudice based on ignorance or racial bias. It is a political contradiction that nonetheless defines how we perceive ourselves and others. Race, whether absurd or not, permeates aspects of public discourse and private identity formation. Because the problem of racial injustice is the central fact of black-white relations in America, race operates as a critique of society that is grounded in how an individual chooses to incorporate her collective past. As a marker of the American cultural past and an ever-present reality of American life, race is about more than social stigma or ascribed identity. Race is a profoundly meaningful social difference that can simultaneously stigmatize and nurture personal growth and political resistance.

Factoring how an individual or group conceptualizes race across all the domains described in the model allows theorists to explain the complexities of racial difference. Because race is a meta-reality of confluence and contradiction, factoring it across each of the relevant arenas provides useful information about the ethical, social, and political consequences of group identity.

Class is also a pervasive marker of social relations. Although class distinctions provide important information about the relationship between individuals and groups, they often obscure the possession and use of power by those designated as poor or working-class. Class is a social category that hierarchically defines social relations in a capitalist economy. Class locates groups around the dynamics of this hierarchy and situates the individual within various communities. In this sense, community objectifies class relations, and class is therefore an aspect of community.

Feminist theorists can use the relational model of difference to theorize race as a gendered reality and gender as an integral part of the problem of race. With a stronger conceptual basis for women's differences, feminists can then create authentic discourse and support effective political action.

III

Each major strand of second-wave feminist theory limited the goals and aspirations of women of color. For that reason, black women challenged the theoretical assumptions and the social implications of second-wave thought. Because of the undisputed truth and pain of being excluded by white feminists, black feminists forged a protest tradition that served as the conscience of the feminist movement but couldn't overcome the imposition of false standards of racial inclusion. Thus, the movement included women of color without reexamining its theoretical frameworks in light of these women's experiences. As a result, the politics of black feminist protest within the white feminist movement prevented black feminist theorizing from understanding the decline of black women's empowerment. This separation made it impossible for black feminists in the second wave to anticipate and respond to the new realities of race and gender in America. Moreover, protesting black exclusion from the feminist mainstream marginally privileged a few feminist writer-activists but spurred many other black feminist intellectuals to abandon local activism.

Of course, not all black feminists curtailed their community work. For example, many organized around issues of sexual aggression, including rape and domestic violence. But neither the organizing nor the cogent analyses of black sexuality by such writers as Angela Davis, Paula Giddings, Darlene Clark Hine, and Patricia Hill Collins have produced a general theory of race and sex aggression that can provide a framework for understanding the crisis of black womanhood and its impact on black communities.

Sex aggression and the control of black sexuality suppress black women's desire for intimacy and their capacity for personal and collective growth. Yet the inability of black feminists to develop a coherent discourse of black sexual development perpetuates the silence regarding the sexual terrorism experienced by black women. The suppressed rage and violence behind racist images of black sexuality continue to place limits on genuine black sexual expression.

Because second-wave black feminists raised their issues in the context of socialist or radical left-wing politics, they misread the social implications of the rapid and devastating changes in the historical, political, cultural, and economic context of the black communities they purported to represent. Because the black feminist struggle operated within the narrow confines of Afrocentric national-ism and mainstream feminism, it not only failed to empower black women but actually led to a decline in black women's activism.

This decline of black women's empowerment is characterized by a diminution of black women's grassroots activism. Black women's abdication of community building and political action repudiates standards of black womanhood that pre-vious generations were socialized to uphold. A series of public attacks ruptured the connection between black women and their traditional socialization. The dis-connection between black women and their historic identity means that black women continue to struggle with gender expectations that force them to choose be-tween personal fulfillment and sexual desire, between intimacy and social commit-ment, between materialism and freedom, between gender and race. The inability of many black women to reconcile their individual aspirations with their collec-tive needs is part of the continuing legacy of the crisis of black womanhood.

IV

History and enmity impaled black feminists on the horns of three impossible challenges. The first challenge was the need to prove to other black women that feminism was not for white women only. Confronting white feminists with the demand to share power and to affirm diversity was the second challenge. The third challenge involved fighting the misogynist tendencies of black nationalism.

The fact that black feminists had to expend so much energy to change the terms of the feminist debate shows how entrenched racism was within second-wave feminism. Yet despite major shortcomings, the contributions that black women made to the feminist debate cannot be ignored. Black feminists were in the forefront in legitimately demanding that issues of diversity be addressed within the movement to end gender oppression. Black feminist writing con-tributed to this important directional shift in several ways, by

- providing critiques of black nationalism and white feminism;
- documenting black women's contributions to African American writing and activism as well as to the major social movements of American history;
- creating an accurate historical record of black women's creative and in-tellectual contributions to American letters and American life;
- analyzing black gender oppression in terms of race and class;
- giving voice to black women's creativity and spirituality;
- keeping issues of poverty and economic exploitation before a largely in-different public.

Black feminist writings demanded alternatives to existing social arrangements and were committed to working toward new visions for women and community. Rather than framing their arguments for inclusion in the movement or in society at large as pleas from outcasts, black feminists challenged feminism and the American body politic to recognize the strength of black women as a force for economic opportunity and racial justice.

Despite these achievements, the disconnection between black feminist theorizing and black women's lives choked off ordinary black women's community activism. Although black women remain active in a wide range of social, cultural, religious, political, business, and educational organizations, many black communities experienced a decline in local activism from which they have yet to recover.

The failures of black feminism must be viewed in the context of what was achieved. However, at a time when new challenges confront black women and black communities, it is important to understand both the uses and limits of feminism in terms of its impact on black women. Understanding this history is a necessary step in the resurgence of black women's empowerment.

3. Gender and Community: The Power of Transcendence

I am an invisible man. No, I am not a spook like those who haunted Edgar Allan Poe; nor am I one of your Hollywood movie ectoplasms. I am a man of substance, of flesh, and bone, fiber and liquids and I might even be said to possess a mind. I am invisible, understand, simply because people refuse to see me. . . . When they approach me they see only my surroundings, themselves, or figments of their imagination—indeed, everything and anything except me.

—Ralph Ellison, *Invisible Man*

Despite both penetrating and pedantic discussions of race in America, few pundits or intellectuals have effectively addressed, in practical political terms, the seemingly intractable problems of poverty, unemployment, poor education, violence, and drugs among poor blacks. Although feminist research has contributed to America's understanding of its racial problems, it is increasingly clear that ending racism and economic dislocation will require organizing for progressive social change. This is especially true for black women, whose political activism could mobilize key constituencies within black communities. In this context, it is necessary to connect the implications of a decline in black women's empowerment to the needs of black children, especially poor black children. Social conservatives exploit issues of children and family as part of their agenda. In response to their usurpation of family values, black women who support a more humane and more inclusive approach to families will play a significant role in the creation of a new black political agenda. This chapter discusses why this is so.

I

With riveting agony like that of an electric shock, poor black children—long ago, at somewhere between the ages of ten and fifteen, and today, at as young as two or three—are painfully jolted to find that their place in the world is with the despised. Long before many black children know why and what it all means, they get two lethal messages from society at large. The first is that they simply don't count. For a myriad of interconnected social reasons that everyone is hard-pressed to explain, poor black children learn early that they do not exist in the broader world and that nothing they will ever do or think is of the slightest consequence to anything that really matters.

The second message poor kids get, even more devastating than the first, is that the only self they are expected to build is one that will discount them. These children, continuously assaulted by the inadequacy of themselves and their kind, are denied permission to build a joyous sense of who they really are. They are not expected to construct healthy answers to questions of role, responsibility, dignity, or beauty; they are not expected to understand what it is to be human except through what is presented to them as deserved deprivation.

Most white people's views of blacks in general and poor blacks in particular are nightmarish combinations of half-truths and lies, mixed with fear and fantasy. For too many black children, this nightmare is all there is. They become trapped in other people's fears, and over time they begin to see everything around them as pure, unrelenting distortion. Like a newspaper for the nearsighted reader without glasses, reality is a washed-out, continuous blur whose meaning is never fully understood. This feeling slowly enrages the children.

Then there are the voices, the mind's demonic sounds, the internal wailing, groans, sighs, mocking laughter, and echoed whispers—desperate sounds that burst forth inside the walls of children's minds, droning, "They're right," "You don't matter," "You can't do it," "You aren't important." These words accompany every challenge and compromise every opportunity the children receive. Self-doubt lingers and is often fulfilled. After a time, these sounds drown out everything else, so that eventually the children can hear nothing of their own voices.

I am one of those people—perhaps you are too—who judges a society by how it treats its children, especially its poor children.[1] If watching how a society cares for children, especially poor ones, provides glimpses of its moral capital, then America is one of many bankrupt nations. Consider that children are the poorest group in America. They represent 40 percent of the people in the United States who live below poverty, yet they are just over 25 percent of the population. Consider also that twenty-three other developed nations have lower infant mortality rates than the United States does.[2]

Too little has been written about how today's poor black boys and girls respond to the messages I have described. For much of the nation, these children and their parents are distant, invisible, and shrouded in evil and misery. But as part of our efforts to reduce child poverty, the country needs to get much more specific about how today's messages of black inferiority influence poor children's sense of manhood and womanhood. We need to sort out what we know from what we don't know. For example, we know that poor boys and girls are more likely to join gangs out of a need for both protection and recognition. Social scientists also tell us that black boys engage in violent behavior more often than girls largely because they see too few positive black male role models. Youth workers convincingly describe how black girls receive numerous invisible blows to their sexual development. The workers contend that this occurs primarily because the developmental needs of black girls are frequently erased in discussions about black youths that center on the problems of young, delinquent black boys or pregnant black girls—the two subgroups of black youths that whites find so troubling. However, scientists, philanthropists, educators, and youth workers cannot seem to share enough of what they know about how today's poor black boys and girls who aren't killing each other or becoming parents too soon cope with a stigmatized identity. As a nation, we need to focus on whatever resources these kids have or are able to acquire so that we can replicate their successes.

Scholars and practitioners must help us understand how our children deal with the stigma of poverty and the close association of that stigma with race. If our society really examined this question, it would be drawn back into the history and traditions of black communities. We know how past generations learned to confront and often to defeat race degradation. This knowledge could be helpful in understanding today's social problems. For example, we know that one important value that was stressed historically in black communities was helping each other. Joanne and Elmer Martin define a black helping tradition as a form of collective action against racial degradation. They see this tradition as the primary strategy for coping with racism: "In examining the black helping tradition, we propose that it developed from the black extended family's struggles against patriarchy and its emphasis on mutual aid and cooperation among members of different social classes or status groups.... We further propose that... the black helping tradition spread into practically every phase of black community life" (1985, 2). The Martins describe the socialization of children as part of an African cultural heritage passed from generation to generation: "Children were brought up to take on the pro-social ways of their elders.... Children learned the habit of helping their parents and worked under the system of reciprocity of/with other people" (14). The helping tradition was therefore part of a black child's socialization.

Given a strong understanding of our cultural past, we really need to know whether and how much the helping tradition anchors the socialization of today's poor black children. Although such norms have greatly diminished, they still exist. If we want more poor children to nullify the effects of racial degradation, the question becomes, how can America rebuild helping traditions within all black communities?

Of course, despite the black community's amazing legacy of coping behaviors, we know that there have been far too many casualties among those who dwell invisibly amid social oppression. Marita Bonner, a black woman writer in the 1920s, describes the atmosphere and the attitude of those who live among the casualities of neglect:

> If you have never lived among your own, you feel prodigal. Some warm untouched current flows through them—through you and drags you out into the deep water of a new sea of human foibles and mannerisms; of a peculiar psychology and prejudices. And one day you find yourself entangled—enmeshed—pinioned in the seaweed of a Black Ghetto. Not a Ghetto placid like the Strasse that flows, outwardly unperturbed and calm...but a peculiar group. Cut off, flung together, shoved aside in a bundle because of color and with no more in common.... Milling around like live fish in a basket. Those at the bottom crushed into a sort of stupid apathy by the weight of those on the top. Those on top leaping, leaping, leaping to scale the sides to get out. ([1925] 1991, 26)

There is no romance, no nostalgia, and little hope if you're at the bottom of the barrel. Bonner's description is poignant, despite her obvious disdain for the masses that arises, perhaps, from a curious and unique combination of relative privilege and inchoate racial anger. Her words capture the reality of black life for children who must make choices from what little is made available to them. Racism demands so much from its victims that we should never be surprised by the large number of casualties and should always be surprised that so many people escape.

Against the crude survival mentality and the senseless death of today's ghetto, we know that past generations responded by developing positive alternatives to being despised. Alternatives to living stigmatized and ashamed were predicated on a will to resist that black people transmitted across generations. Apparently, the will to resist being totally defined by white racism is a key aspect of being black that all black children need to understand. This seems to suggest that black people need to pay more attention to the processes involved in socializing black children.

Living black in white America involves acquiring a set of valuable social skills, including the need to help one another and the will to resist. In generations past, these skills were given to children first by those closest to them—their mothers, fathers, and extended family—and then by others who genuinely valued them. Within the black cultural system, the role of other-mothers, black male role models, and ordinary people was to teach values and to strengthen the will.

Black children were taught that they could use very little of society's definitions in the construction of their identities. A child was exposed to the mysteries of white prejudice and was taught how to survive them through informal contact with family, friends, and community people, as well as through formal contact with black-controlled institutions or with blacks who secured and maintained pockets of control within white institutions. Black teachers, preachers, youth workers, coaches, and volunteers, among others, dedicated significant time and money to helping children express race pride so that they understood that their futures were not totally bound by white injustice and ridicule. Members of the black community would oversee the process of helping children construct self-identities independent of the nightmarish illusions created by the dominant culture. The children were taught that a strong and principled self-identity repudiated the notion of black inferiority. This defiant rejection was encouraged so that a child might alter her position in relation to the dominant culture, allowing her to create her own space. Children understood that creating their own spaces meant being in control of themselves and seeing themselves as capable of organizing their experiences around important values and goals rather than around white people's views of how much they did or didn't count.

Given this discussion, it seems that the most important thing about the black community, which, as Bonner and others have written, can be regressive and stifling, is its capacity to nurture positive self-definition. In the past, communities were places of nurture created by parents, other adults, peers, siblings, and community leaders to be safe havens in a hostile world.

In fact, black people, whether brutalized by the plantation or by the urban ghetto, built community as an essential part of the cultural survival skills they received from an African past. In community, parents and other leaders nurtured the young and protected them until presumably they incorporated a will to resist the perceptions of a world that despised them. My parents, like most in their generation, experienced the brutality of racism and the scarification of the psyche it creates. But despite these experiences, or perhaps because of them, my parents and countless other black parents transmitted cultural knowledge about the power of self-definition. Children received these messages whether or not they were fortunate enough to have "good parents." It was a responsibility of the community as a whole to teach and protect them. To create community, nurture children, and strengthen the will to resist, blacks told stories with pointed themes of racial contradiction. They also created positions of responsibility within black institutions, supported extended families, built economic institutions, and engaged in organized protest to extend the benefits of positive self-definition to collective action.

I use the term *transcendence* to characterize cultural behaviors involved in moving the subjugated self beyond degradation. This term has been used by Simone de Beauvoir, among others, to describe the fundamental nature of human existence. Although in *The Second Sex* de Beauvoir does not specifically define transcendence, she states: "Every individual concerned to justify... his existence feels that [this justification] involves an undefined need to transcend himself, to engage in freely chosen projects" ([1953] 1974, 77). Racism makes every black person "concerned to justify his [or her] existence." So every black person who has any hope of survival must transcend not only in the sense that de Beauvoir implies, by moving the self beyond the limits of human mortality, but also in the way that I use the term, by moving the self beyond the social, cultural, spiritual, and psychological limitations imposed by the dominant culture.

In my view, the idea of transcendence requires a much higher level of existence than that implied by the civil rights mantra "We shall overcome." This is not a criticism of overcoming, which I acknowledge is necessary to defeat racism as well as gender and class oppression. However, overcoming is not the only tool that oppressed people have historically used to defeat stigmatized identities. Overcoming a barrier implies struggling against a significant and seemingly immovable object that stands between us and our individual and collective aspirations. The only question worth asking under such circumstances is, how long? Transcendence, by contrast, reframes the circumstance and reconfigures our encounter with the obstacle, freeing us to ask an entirely new set of questions, such as, how come? and who said so? and who else? These questions challenge the implicit social arrangements enforced by the master class. Asking these questions therefore creates alternatives to simply enduring racial, gender, class, or community degradation. Overcoming struggles against oppression; transcendence changes the material basis of oppression and opens up new possibilities. Transcendence places our individual and collective power in the foreground and shifts the focus from the oppressor to the collective resources available to defeat oppression.

The crucial difference between overcoming and transcendence is that overcoming places the challenge that must be defeated right in the center of our consciousness. This gives the object of our despair enormous power, like a fifty-car freight train that lumbers along as you wait before the lowered gates of the rail crossing, oblivious to you and the appointment that you're late for.

Transcendence, especially as it operated in historical black communities, became a state of consciousness available to the entire community. It released the enormous power of kin, clan, and spirit that made it possible to cope with racism by transforming it. Transcendence placed everything people knew and believed about themselves, about who they were, where they'd been, and where they were going, at the center of their consciousness. Transcendence meant that everything one knew about race was filtered through a consciousness fortified by countless self-defining moments connected by history and tradition to the wisdom of one's ancestors. Although the power of transcendence never increased the speed of the freight train or made time stand still as the train moved, it did reduce the train's impact on the rest of one's life. This occurred precisely because the train ceased to be the center of attention, and therefore one was free to use the waiting time more productively.

Black parents and black people in the community prepared my generation for transcendence. They prepared us, sometimes lovingly and sometimes harshly but always out of compassion, to defeat racism. They knew that their children had to engage racial hatred at a whole different level if they were going to reclaim the dignity that is the rightful possession of every human being.

Black transcendence does not originate inside the self. It is not biologically determined, and although it requires an individual act of will, it is not acquired simply by individual volition. In other words, black people do not transcend their negation and invisibility exclusively as a result of their individual capabilities or aspirations. Although it is true that black achievement results from individual effort, the spirit of transcendence is a cultural legacy. It is one of the most valuable gifts of black culture and black life.

Transcendence, then, is not simply the consequence of an individual's ability to beat the odds. This point is especially important because too many black parents are mistakenly teaching their children to become complacent in the face of a perverse form of social Darwinism. This social complacency and fear of rocking the boat motivates children toward individual achievement and away from group identity, responsibility, and collective action. Children are not being taught the power of transcendence. They learn to make career connections, do deals, and engage in social climbing rather than how to build and nurture relationships with people. Too many black children are not being taught that transcendence is a cultural legacy that ultimately requires self-acceptance and a faith in oneself and one's clan. This legacy is honored and known more completely than the reality of racism, gender oppression, class difference, or social isolation.

All children need to be taught that life is to be lived using certain tools: faith, values, discipline, perseverance, respect, harmony, sacrifice, and service. Black children need to become conscious of the forces that seek to make them invisible or to isolate them from their own cultural traditions. They need to be taught to resist the forces that negate ethnic pride and racial uplift. Black children need to understand their culture and to accept it as a source of power without embracing racial chauvinism. As blacks strive for acceptance in the American mainstream, they sometimes negate the value of their collective identity. They experience the fissures and internal contradictions within the black community that often make it difficult for some blacks to feel at home with their own. Despite the tyranny of group norms that contribute to the cruel and ignorant suppression of individual aspirations, there is no doubt that black men and women in previous generations built black communities to teach today's adults to help each other. When black parents teach their children to value individualism over collective action, they perpetuate a stigmatizing view of race that locks the collective movement of our feet in step with those who despise what God made us to be.

Although transcendence is probably part of the cultural development of all oppressed people, Africans and African Americans have a special relationship to the idea. The vitality of black transcendence is self-definition that promotes the welfare of both the individual and the community. Black transcendence involves racial uplift and ethnic pride. Racial uplift stresses values such as education, service, protest, and self-help to promote the improvement of the race (Martin and Martin, 1985, 5). Ethnic pride stresses respect and honor for black people who exemplify these values. Black transcendence uses many modalities for self-expression and community building: music, fine and decorative arts, color, light, expressiveness, and style—all cultural elements of transcendence. Physicality is also part of transcendence. Physical activity such as sports, skilled trades, and manual labor brings the body into harmony with nature through artistic expression. Anyone who has ever watched Michael Jordan go to the hoop or Paul Robeson sing a Negro work song knows exactly what I mean.

But regrettably, as we witness the dawn of a new age, blacks are in danger of losing both the helping tradition and the ability to balance independent self-definition with collective responsibility. Concern over the loss of such a valuable source of strength for African Americans requires a deeper discussion of the state of black America.

II

Black America is still fundamentally confused about what should be done to ensure the future of the race. Even after surviving, overcoming, marching, singing, waving weapons, and other forms of holding white folks' feet to the fire on issues of race, black people still suffer the effects of racism.

What is important about this observation is not that blacks are oppressed — this, after all, has been the case almost since the first white person set foot on African soil. What is different about this period in black history is that no dominant paradigm has emerged from the black community about how to solve the problem of race in America. Race-based and non-race-based solutions bitterly compete for ascendancy. Yet the political agency needed to effect any solution is fragmented and weak. As a result, competing class interests, divergent needs and aspirations, lingering doubts about our collective worth, the unrelenting bashing of black life in the media, and the commercialization of black culture have produced a lack of consensus regarding which political strategies are appropriate today.

In short, blacks lack a clear agenda for reducing the effects of racism. Today's race leaders recognize that their success depends on helping blacks to create new forms of cross-class and cross-race political solidarity in the face of changing demographics and more insidious forms of race and class oppression. Black leaders, however, have not clearly defined the case for black activism and have therefore experienced limited success in promoting race solidarity across social classes.

The conservative black middle class views the racial barriers that exist for poor blacks as instances of internalized stigma. Too many middle-class blacks believe that poor blacks see themselves as victims and that their behavior and belief in their own worthlessness are more consequential than the existence of race prejudice in accounting for their lack of achievement. After all, race, although treated as stigmatizing, is essentially a rather arbitrary and often meaningless way to categorize human variation, so it would seem natural that to leave behind racial stigma would be to promote the bootstrap mentality and Judeo-Christian work ethic that some successful blacks claim is the solution to the problem of race. These blacks have overcome Jim Crow and operate under the assumption that transcending race involves moving beyond the need for race solidarity. In

other words, these blacks deny the impact of race so that it can impose no obligation on them as upwardly mobile individuals to advance others in their group.

A main reason why black people are so divided on the issue of race is that
they are very conflicted about the meaning of race and very aware of the limits
of racial collective action. Black people know how to overcome barriers to race
as they were defined during the civil rights era; but the accomplishments of having overcome are so far below black expectations that many black people doubt
the efficacy of collective action.

Black Americans are often too beleaguered and too busy with their individual
aspirations to teach black children the power of transcendence. Instead, many
blacks send the message that their children should accept their racial heritage
but do nothing to advance it. If the children are poor, they are allowed to believe
that racism is so powerful an enemy that they bear no responsibility for being
isolated, degraded, or ignored. Middle-class youths are becoming less prepared
each day to meet the challenges of racism, and poor kids know only the stigma
attached to being black.

III

Within the broader context of the failure of blacks to prepare today's generation
to cope with being black in America, there are at least five major reasons why
large numbers of blacks are failing to pass on the vital knowledge of transcendence. The first reason for the loss of our power to transcend is directly related
to the lingering negativity between black men and black women. In America,
black men and women are often invisible to the larger society. Judging, however,
by the sometimes palpably hostile relationships between black men and women,
being invisible is easier than having our sexuality apprehended as part of a white
nightmare of racial stereotypes and fantasies.[3]

The broader society's images of black sexuality rarely acknowledge the fact
that black people have loving relationships and families. For this reason, black men
and women should celebrate rather than equivocate about their connections to
each other. Black men and women will always be connected by the continent of
Africa—the wondrous, tortured, splendid motherland in all its pain and glory.
We are drawn to each other by a common ethnic past, a common cultural legacy,
and a common need to resist the cruelties of white supremacy. Even when black
men and black women are not bonded by sexual intimacy, when they are not
bonded by progeny, when they are not bonded by tradition, they are still connected to each other both by African ancestry and by the invisibility and negation imposed by racism. If black men reject black women, if they do not prefer

us as sexual partners, do not see our brown bodies as objects of desire, and do not connect to themselves through us, it is because they see us through the eyes of the dominant culture.

When looked at through those eyes, black women wither. Through those eyes we are seen as the ones who deserve to be used, abused, negated, and erased. Through those eyes, we are the only ones upon whom the black man can exact vengeance as a male prerogative. Through those eyes, black women are doubly disgraced and thoroughly vulnerable, scorned because we sleep with, parent, and try to build lives with men whom white intellectuals—social scientists, policy makers, journalists, and ordinary Americans—fear or deem worthless. We bear witness to hapless rage and stand ashamed as our lovers and sons struggle not to despise us because we lived in the master's house and were forced to do his sexual bidding. Black women endure love turned to loathing because we suckled Master's children or worked in Miss Anne's kitchen and brought home her table scraps for our children to eat. We bear the anger because our men had to disappear in order for the family to get welfare and because we survived a system not of our own choosing.

The fear, power, and potential of these intimate connections are obscured by the evil of white supremacy and the stigma of color consciousness, both of which are linked to a history of white access to and control of black sexuality. The sexual mythology and the legacy of white power over black sexuality intervene between black men and women who, as a result, have the added burden of defining their sexual identities in contrast to those imposed by the dominant culture. Unfortunately, the stigma of race still has the power to cause black men and women to displace anger about racism from the racists to each other. Under these circumstances, it is not surprising that black women are seen as a source of black male oppression.

Black men and women working together to repair the damage that they have inflicted on each other because of generations of sexual pain and abuse is a necessary prerequisite to restoring black transcendence. Black people must forgive themselves for being forced to live together with each other's despair. Building strong relationships with each other as we restore the fabric of collective life is necessary if blacks are to guarantee the availability of transcendence for future generations.

The second reason for the loss of black transcendence is economic. I use the term *economic* in a much broader sense than that of whether or not blacks have jobs. The increasing concentration of wealth, the movement of capital, and the globalization of class oppression are the price the world pays for irresponsible commodity consumption. As the gap between black people with money and those without it continues to widen, class conflict will escalate as political interests diverge. Eurocentric economic policies are exacerbating class, racial, and ethnic tensions around the world, especially in countries heedlessly involved in the creation of market economies. Diverging class interests replicated worldwide will make it increasingly difficult for marginalized groups to identify their real collective self-interest, because dominant groups will ruthlessly suppress such identification. These new economic realities require new strategies for promoting economic opportunity and group solidarity. Black people will need to advocate for domestic and international economic policies that are essential to a range of black social and economic interests.

The third reason for the loss of transcendence in the black community is that African American cultural development is currently dominated by bourgeois and street values. These values undermine community as a basis for African American collective action. Although the black middle class and the black poor are deeply suspicious of each other, one common thread connects them. Both bourgeois and street values stress individualism and see money and material possessions as important indicators of self-worth.

Although the hardworking black bourgeoisie has historically been a source of race leaders and racial uplift, it has always vacillated between improving the social status and condition of relatively privileged blacks and working to create wider social and economic opportunities for all black people. Although members of the bourgeoisie like to see themselves as victims punished by other blacks for wanting to get ahead,[4] their claims of being rejected by their own for not acknowledging race as a barrier to individual achievement mask the predatory and frequently unprincipled nature of their pursuits. Moreover, the black middle class — the basic pool from which the vast majority of cultural leadership is drawn — often chooses to see nothing good in poor black people. Similarly, poor and working-class blacks often despise the bourgeoisie. They feel betrayed by and isolated from a civil society that they know either ignores or exploits them.

The predatory nature of street culture brings me to the fourth reason for the loss of transcendence, namely, the social disorder rampant in low-income black communities. Street culture promotes anarchy. Black leadership is often perplexed by and ashamed of the senseless violence surrounding life in the inner city. Black leaders who directly try to confront the menace of poverty and the breakdown of civil society in poor black communities must continuously struggle against white antipathy, black conspiracy theories, irresponsible media coverage, and opportunistic opinion makers who define issues of crime, family violence, premarital sex, and the prevalence of gangs, drugs, violence, teen pregnancy, child abuse, and neglect as social problems that involve only urban blacks. In the current political climate, the social anarchy in inner-city black communities overshadows the organizing and direct action that are being done to mitigate the effects of poverty. The drugs, violence, guns, and crime that are almost exclusively associated with the black urban ghetto are used to indict not only liberal-style social programs but also black people as a group.

The problem of social decline of low-income black communities relates to the fifth reason why these neighborhoods are not places of nurture and transcendence. Simply stated, black women's involvement in community-based political action has declined, and this decline is, in part, the result of a crisis of black womanhood. The loss of black transcendence is related to political repression and social policies that have devalued black women's traditional responsibility to sustain cultural resistance within the fabric of community life. Black transcendence is significantly dependent on the power of active black women who have been socialized to act as agents of political action and social cohesion. Stripped of this traditional role as culture bearers, community builders, and change agents, too many black women reject traditional standards of black womanhood. Too many middle-class black women pursue their career interests and claim that their privileges, special talents, or past contributions absolve them from the responsibilities of community building. Community-building roles have been jettisoned by a broad segment of black women who no longer feel obligated to create caring black communities.

Politically conservative explanations for black social decline such as racial inferiority or the lack of personal responsibility on the part of low-income blacks are much more appealing to the dominant culture than is an attempt to understand the effects of racism defined in terms of economic exploitation, political apathy, and gender denigration. After all, racist explanations of black social decline are much simpler and more direct than the convoluted, equivocating, and indirect messages of many leaders and intellectuals. The simple idea of black inferiority affirms European hegemony and connects centuries of Eurocentric xenophobia to newer and more insidious forms of race prejudice. But the real explanations for the social pathology within black communities involve culpability on the part of both black and white people, and that pathology will require major investments of time, creativity, and other resources to reverse.

The assault on black womanhood and the diminished power of black communities to help children transcend racism represent a significant challenge to black women. However, many engaged and committed local activists are successfully addressing these problems. Based on their successes, black women activists know that the time has come to reach wider groups of people with alternatives to conservative models of social change. To this end, black feminists should engage other women activists and join national efforts to help mobilize on behalf of black children, families, and communities. Together, black feminists and activists can broaden the commitment to progressive political change.

Black women need to return to forgotten communities all over America and to do what it takes to give each of our children the power of transcendence. As black women restore transcendence as an integral part of black cultural development and community life, they will reaffirm the values inherent in black feminist theorizing.

Because black women are the purveyors of the power of transcendence, they have a mandate to address the needs of the black community. Focusing gender and racial uplift on black culture and black community will connect black women to their history and help them to reclaim their destiny. The most important reason for this journey is what is at stake. To nurture black children in the ways of transcendence requires that black women create a new gender consciousness, one that actively seeks progressive social change. Black children need this now more than ever.

4. The Crisis of Black Womanhood

Historically, the black woman . . . has had to work alongside the black man in a struggle unlike that of any other group in the United States. For black people have had to hack their way through the wilderness of racism embedded by nearly four centuries of a barbarous international slave trade, two centuries of chattel slavery and a century of struggle to achieve full citizenship even after the Emancipation Proclamation. Hers has been a desperate effort to make a place of dignity for her people. . . . Not only have these women stood shoulder to shoulder with black men in every phase of the battle, but they have continued to stand when their men have been destroyed by it.

> **—Dorothy Height, "Testimony before the New York City Commission on Human Rights"**

Women have been hosts for fear, doubt, and depression which has immobilized them and urged them to resist the necessary moves to correct what's not working in our lives or in our world.

> **—Susan L. Taylor, "Perspective,"** *Essence* **magazine**

I

Toni Cade Bambara, Michele Wallace, Kesho Yvonne Scott, and Hortense Spillers, among others, have discussed the negative images of black womanhood embodied in the myth of matriarchy and its attendant twin mythologies: the myth of the castrating black bitch and the myth of the superwoman (Bambara, 1970; Wallace, 1979; Scott, 1991; Spillers, 1984). Few have discussed what happened to move black women from Dorothy Height's description in 1970 to Susan Taylor's in 1991. What caused black women to become immobilized? Why are black women resisting the "necessary moves to correct what's not working in [their] lives"? What, in short, is the cause of the present crisis of black womanhood? What strategies can black women develop to respond positively to the situations, challenges, and circumstances in their lives? What can motivate black women to take collective action to strengthen each other across social class and to have a political impact on the people and the issues they care about?

To answer these questions, it is important to understand that Taylor's comment is not an isolated occurrence; rather, it describes a particular rupture in black women's gender identity. This disruption of historical patterns of black womanhood is the aftermath of a subtle but relentless attack on the traditions of black female gender consciousness. The attack and its aftermath have been called a crisis because the situation is unprecedented, pervasive, and far-reaching (Radford-Hill, 1986). Moreover, the root cause of this disconnection between historical forms of black gender socialization and today's loss of black women's empowerment is beyond the capacity of individual women to solve.

Crisis is an overused term. From a crisis at the White House to the next crisis in our nation's schools, from the periodic crisis in the world economy to the ongoing crisis in the Middle East, times of instability, danger, and impending doom are becoming almost routine. Given this context, merely explaining the crisis of black womanhood is not enough. In any turning point in history, people often wall off their emotions to separate their psyches from perpetual pain. This has been especially true for black women, who are forbidden to reflect on themselves and each other. We are encouraged to be strong and stay strong. We are encouraged to erect a fire wall between life and its miseries, between us and our vulnerabilities. This wall and our faith are our means of making it through.

But when we simply jettison the pain, bury the shame, and hide the confusion of our disappointments, the power of our emotions becomes unavailable for healing use. It is necessary, therefore, to understand that both the emotional and the intellectual aspects of the crisis are part of the continuing aftermath of gender issues that the civil rights and black power movements left unresolved (Hine and Thompson, 1998). The crisis occurred in part because, in the wake of these movements, segments of the black community, including some black feminists, negated the idea that black women have a responsibility to preserve and renew black culture and to build the black community. Thus, the crisis of black womanhood is both a crisis of political identity and a crisis of belief. The crisis of identity requires an active reassessment of the value of social activism as a vehicle for personal growth and group advancement. The crisis of belief reflects the profound disappointment of a generation whose coming of age witnessed the limits of race-based political action.

The continuing unresolved gender issues within the black community fragment black women's motivations and commitments. Marshaling new and organized efforts to defeat the apathy and complacency that cause black political inaction involves tapping the resilience found in today's black women. Reclaiming the power of our history can restore the spirit of community and encourage seemingly defeated individuals to set positive expectations for themselves and their families.

Ultimately, the crisis reflects black women's ambivalence toward the value of maintaining ethnic community. This ambivalence reflects the constraints that family and career place on political action, as well as the frustrations of reconciling the social, economic, and political differences of divergent class interests and needs. When black women equivocate about the value of their communities and about their roles in maintaining them, they erode the development of their political culture. Unfortunately, black women are encouraged to ignore this political erosion.

In an era of high-profile, megasuccessful black women who are changing the face of every major field worldwide, it's easy to declare victory and to dismiss the continuing need for race and gender consciousness. It is also easy to ignore black women whose individual and collective aspirations are thwarted by low-wage employment, domestic violence, addiction, child abuse, and a host of other self-defeating behaviors and relationships. When the general society pays attention to these women, they are often portrayed as examples of moral decline rather than as symptoms of black political dysfunction.

It is commonly believed that the loss of social cohesion among African Americans is a consequence of ending legal discrimination in America and of expanding the black middle class, whose obligation to the race declined with its increased access to the social and economic mainstream. An equally crucial but rarely discussed cause for the decline in ethnic solidarity is the deterioration of black women's political culture. This loss of political infrastructure and organizing is connected to the inability of black women to define and promote social roles that incorporate traditional standards of black womanhood.

II

More than three decades of devaluing black women's traditional gender identity have resulted in the decline of black women's political activism. Regardless of social class, black women often seem unable to sustain community through political action. Understanding how political immobilization relates to this rupture of black female identity requires an understanding of the political activism of black women in the 1960s.

In this pivotal decade when the crisis began, young black women were idealistic foot soldiers determined to kill first Jim and then Jane Crow. Their unprecedented numbers and strident demands for social change made these young women fundamentally different, so they thought, from their mothers, who grew up in the 1940s.

The black teens and young adults of the 1960s absorbed the heady, optimistic "young, gifted, and black" spirit of the times. Protests were filled with freedom songs, political slogans, and social ideals. Black people began walking in Montgomery but were soon "marchin' up to Freedom Land." Freedom rides, civil rights, the March on Washington, Free Africa, voting rights, the worldwide liberation struggle, and black power all changed America.

In the world of popular culture, Aretha Franklin was the undisputed queen of soul, and young black men and women were insisting on "R-E-S-P-E-C-T." Hordes of young black people pursued whatever they pursued with a decided disdain for their Uncle Tomming elders and an increasing regard for poor, uneducated, and unsophisticated blacks in urban centers or rural towns. These brothers and sisters were oppressed, but somehow they hadn't succumbed, hadn't sold out, hadn't been anything or anyone other than black folk.

Young men and women claimed their lost African heritage. After centuries of being "coloreds" and decades of being Negroes, having been made to feel ashamed of our ancestry for more than 350 years, we were finally proud. We sang "(Say It Loud) I'm Black and I'm Proud," because James Brown and his music captured the feeling that our true destiny had arrived.

To strengthen their connection to the motherland, some black men and women changed their names. Almost overnight, Frank, Christine, John, and Nadine became Adewale, Sheriat, Olatunde, and Oniqa. Many of us kept our slave names but stopped straightening our hair. Black moms all over America were heard saying, "Child, what happened to your head!" We were proud of our naturally curly, African nappy hair. Our "naturals" meant that we were much more in touch with the future than our parents could ever be.

In the South throughout the sixties, black students were leaving classes and integrating buses, lunch counters, and state legislatures. In the major urban areas of the North, it was "Black power," "Power to the people," and "Burn, baby, burn." In response to police brutality, the Black Panther Party popularized "Self-defense and off the pigs!" Malcolm X, a hero to all those with black pride, broke with the Nation of Islam and founded the Organization for Afro-American Unity, dedicated to freedom by any means necessary.

The older generation watched young blacks wage war against poverty, accommodationist Negroes, the government, and the people in the faraway land of "Viet-NAM." We were young and threatening to the social order, "kids mindin' grown folks' business." As a result, we were placed under surveillance, infiltrated, informed on, beaten, captured, jailed, and killed.

The times were socially extreme, politically naive, and violently repressive. August 1965: The Watts riot began. At least thirty-four people died. October 1967: After stopping Black Panther Huey P. Newton for a traffic violation, Officer John Frey was killed. Newton was convicted of voluntary manslaughter and sentenced to a maximum of fifteen years in prison. April 1968: Martin Luther King Jr. was struck by an assassin's bullet. Race riots in Washington, New York, Chicago, Detroit, and at least one hundred other communities followed as news of King's assassination spread. June 1968: Robert Kennedy was assassinated. Roy Innis became the national director of the Congress of Racial Equality (CORE), and the organization began to advocate separatism. November 1968: Shirley Chisholm was elected the nation's first black congresswoman.

The escalating domestic turmoil mirrored the country's increasing conflict over the Vietnam War: "Hell, no! We won't go!" Young Americans were fighting in the government's undeclared war and fighting against it at the same time. "Jackson State," "Kent State," and "Make love, not war" echoed throughout the nation. The war claimed the lives of more than fifty thousand U.S. troops and thousands of MIAs.

Political repression and death were the price young people paid to the defenders of law and order. Although not all of us were politically repressed, everyone knew what the term meant. Young people rallied on behalf of political prisoners like H. Rap Brown, George Jackson, and Angela Davis. Whether working in the civil rights movement, the Black Panther Party, or the movement to "Free Angela," many young black people learned about counterintelligence programs of the FBI and other organizations, which were used to undermine the civil rights, Black Muslim, black liberation, Puerto Rican independence, antiwar, and radical student movements. Black Panther Party members and supporters loved and mourned leaders Fred Hampton and Mark Clark, who were killed at their residence at 2337 West Monroe Street in Chicago during a police raid organized by Cook County state's attorney Edward V. Hanrahan. Because federal and state governments repressed political activity, many young men and women died—too young and too soon.

III

From a cultural perspective, the crisis of black womanhood would not have been possible without the mass merchandising of consumer products to the baby-boom generation. In the 1950s, the merchandising of black culture began its relentless pursuit of teenagers as a market for consumer goods. Songwriters connected black melodies with rock-and-roll sounds and began the first wave of teen mania. By the mid-fifties, the teenage demand for rock and roll had created the teen love song. These songs eventually propelled black music into the crossover market and onto the pop charts. By the sixties, songwriters added rhythm-and-blues love songs to the rock-and-roll sound, and Motown added a solid formula for the commercial success of black music. This music sustained a teenage cult of romance (Jones, 1980).

Music, lyrics, teen idols, and girl groups were consumer packages that were more suggestive than early television and more available than movies, thanks to cars and transistor radios. Romance ideology began to teach white girls in the sixties that love was more important than anything in the world and would, of course, conquer all. Black girls heard the message too. Teenage heartthrobs had names like Smokey Robinson and the Miracles, Diana Ross and the Supremes, and the Temptations. These groups sang popular love songs like "Baby Love" and "My Girl." Motown made love popular, and revolutionary politics made having love more necessary and making love more desperate.

Girls were encouraged, as they had been in the 1950s, to believe that life began when they met Mr. Right and fell in love. Coming of age in the struggle for civil rights suggested that true love and real equality would be realized in the baby-boom generation. Black women expected personal and collective rewards for their work in the struggle to end segregation. They were extremely disappointed, because their expectations of love and equality were not met.

IV

In 1965, the tide of rising black expectations began to collide with the realities of political resistance. Two major historic events of that year closed the door to early-sixties-style liberal idealism and altered the way black women would be perceived in the struggle for freedom. These events were the publication of Daniel Patrick Moynihan's *The Negro Family: The Case for National Action* and the murder of Malcolm X.

Although Moynihan's report concluded that discrimination and institutional factors led to problems within the Negro family structure, its methodological problems and the political aftermath of its release ultimately placed the cause of Negro inequality in the structure of black families rather than in the unemployment, illiteracy, poverty, and other social ills resulting from the cumulative effects of slavery and race discrimination. After 1965, the civil rights leadership became increasingly tepid and defensive in its response to Moynihan's idea that the matriarchal structure of Negro families was socially deviant and that to fix its effects required resources equivalent to the Marshall Plan that rebuilt Europe after World War II. The Moynihan report raised the specter that blacks would never achieve equality with whites. The burning of Watts in the summer of 1965 somehow seemed to confirm this assessment. In the subsequent debate over the causes of and cures for what ignited Watts, black women and their role within black families and communities were placed at the center of the public-policy response to social deviance among poor black families. Social policy transformed African Americans from a striving but oppressed people to a disadvantaged and powerless minority. This fundamental change was the result of social research and public policy that became fixated on gender and familial relationships among blacks as the sources of black poverty. In the view of many researchers and policy makers, black poverty was caused by the lack of male-dominated households. Therefore, social deviance among blacks was more responsible than race discrimination for black inequality.

Few feminists have explored the gender politics of Malcolm X, but it is possible that had he not been murdered, his disgust with the accommodationist strategies of the civil rights leadership, his willingness to expose the racism behind white analyses of black problems, and his creditability within the black nationalist community might have challenged the notion that the black matriarch was most responsible for deviant black families. Without a serious challenge to this idea, black women were subtly held accountable for the failures of a race whose aspirations were trapped between the failed promises of the War on Poverty and the financial drain of the Vietnam War. Both of these wars are now long past, but the legacy of the myth of black matriarchy stigmatized the gender traditions of black women and, in some ways, created a self-fulfilling prophecy. The aftermath of the cultural trends and social forces that first buffeted black women in the 1960s continues to be felt today.

From Malcolm X's death in February 1965 and the completion of Moynihan's report in March 1965 to the publication of Toni Cade Bambara's *The Black Woman* in 1970, the power of black women as agents for social change was profoundly neutralized. The former two events represent a confluence of factors that contributed to the crisis of black womanhood, including liberal social programs, the shortcomings of second-wave feminism, the macho and misogyny of leftist political activism, the migration of upwardly mobile blacks from traditional black communities to mostly white or integrated suburban communities, and the increasing economic isolation of poor blacks.

The impact of these cultural forces increased gender tensions between African American men and women and contributed to black women's retreat from political activism. The era of social protest was a time of expectation, repression, and sacrifice that ultimately collapsed under the weight of government-sponsored violence and its own naïveté. As a result of theoretical flaws in social ideology and the excesses of leftist politics, Americans began to distance themselves from liberal idealism in the late 1960s and early 1970s. By the mid-seventies, the excessively optimistic social crusades of the sixties had been replaced by various forms of political conservatism. In the 1980s, a self-centered American individualism developed that supported conservative forms of social and economic political action throughout the 1990s.

V

A historical review of black female gender roles reveals how cultural forces existing in the general society led to the crisis of black womanhood. In "The Role of Black Women in the Community of Slaves," Angela Davis defines the purpose of the slave woman's role in the slave community: "The black slave woman... in the infinite anguish of ministering to the needs of the men and children around her, was performing the only labor of the slave community which could not be directly and immediately claimed by the oppressor" (Davis, 1973, 144). Long before Davis's analysis of black women's role in the building of black community, other black women writers identified community building as a source of self-definition (Cooper, 1892). One example of this point is an article by Elsie Johnson McDougald entitled "The Task of Negro Womanhood." This article appeared in *The New Negro,* the famous anthology of Negro art and letters published in 1925. McDougald argues that the nature of black female identity is intimately connected to the needs of the black community:

> We find the Negro woman, figuratively struck in the face daily by contempt from the world about her. Within her soul, she knows little of peace and happiness. But through it all, she is courageously standing erect, developing within herself the moral strength to rise above and conquer false attitudes. She is maintaining her natural beauty and charm and improving her mind and opportunity. She is measuring up to the needs of her family, community, and race, and radiating a hope throughout the land. ([1925] 1977, 382)

A major premise of "The Task of Negro Womanhood" is that the status and condition of the Negro woman can predict the status of the Negro race. To this end,

McDougald lists the hardships, including economic injustice, racial discrimination, and racial stereotypes, that black women of her generation endured. She also clearly delineates the class structure of Negro women in the 1920s. Beginning with the affluent social elite, McDougald describes the contributions of black business and professional women as well as women in the skilled trades and the union movement. At the end of the article, she describes both the oppressive conditions of domestic work and the contributions of the domestic worker. McDougald takes great pride in reciting the achievements and challenges of black women regardless of class status:

> Obsessed with difficulties which might well compel individualism, [the Negro woman] has engaged in a considerable amount of organized action to meet group needs. . . . On the whole, the Negro woman's feminist efforts are directed chiefly toward the realization of the equality of the races, the sex struggle assuming a subordinate place. (381)

McDougald ends her discussion with a direct appeal to improve the status of black women. She recommends that the black community add black women's demands for gender equality to the tradition of racial uplift.

Historically, as these examples illustrate, black women's identity involved upholding community values. This was true despite race prejudice and the inevitable class tensions between blacks who assimilated and those who did not. Black women's socialization embodied a valuable tradition of building community and culture. However, beginning in the 1960s and continuing to the present, this tradition has been harangued out of favor by the social fissures in American culture. These fissures include the aftermath of the Vietnam War, the rise in government-sponsored domestic terrorism, and increased police harassment. They also include liberal demands for changes in black social expectations and gender roles. In essence, the dominant culture's denial of legitimate demands for racial equality even as America dismantled legal segregation made it extremely difficult for black women to adapt traditional roles of self-help and racial uplift. This in turn compromised efforts to assist low-income blacks in communities coping with a variety of social ills.

Moreover, the changes in sex-role expectations that accompanied the demise of legal race discrimination created new ways for black men to define and express their masculinity. Some of the ways that men chose to explore their manhood discounted black women and conflicted with traditional female roles and aspirations. Because black power and antiwar and liberal social protests glorified sexual freedom and warrior masculinity, black men and women experienced unprecedented tensions in their relationships. Today, efforts to build positive and long-lasting relationships between black men and women are still being challenged by the need to reconcile race, identity, and gender expectations with the demands of the broader society.

VI

Throughout the early years of the search for black self-determination, black men adopted the patriarchal traditions of their white counterparts as the standard for black male-female relationships. As a result, black male expectations of black women changed. Many black men began to disparage the egalitarian sex roles that had characterized black gender relationships and sometimes accused black women of dominating and destroying the fabric of the black community. This indictment was predicated on false constructions of familial deviance and female dominance that repudiated black women's traditional gender roles, including mothering, helping, and racial uplifting. Traditionally, black women were socialized to support black families, black communities, and black men. These culture-bearing and community-building roles were essential to black cultural survival. After 1965, this fundamental aspect of black female gender identity was cited by the federal government, as well as the civil rights leadership and the liberal intellectual establishment, as a barrier to the full participation of black men in the economic mainstream. In addition, black nationalists contended that black women's desires for committed relationships and decision-making roles in the nationalist movement were counterrevolutionary.

American domestic policy attempted to cast relationships between black men and women in the image of first liberal and then conservative ideology. The mix of historical events, public policies, and politics began to alter the sexual, social, and economic relationships between black men and women. Moreover, as part of a search for their masculinity in post–Jim Crow America, black men often accepted liberal depictions of black life that stressed deviance and victimization. As a result, they repudiated traditions of black womanhood and began to define racism itself as a loss of black manhood. These men seemed to insist that their right to be treated as men was the sole purpose of revolutionary struggle. Their definitions of masculinity and femininity were hardly revolutionary, however. In fact, nationalist political ideology defined masculinity exactly as it was defined by white men, and for the same purpose: to protect the status quo of gender relations.

As part of the covert domestic war against young people and ethnic minorities, and despite what on the surface appeared to be a commitment to social equality in a Great Society, America supported a subtle yet incendiary counteroffensive to keep blacks subservient to whites. The campaign to destroy left-wing political activism in this country has been well documented (Churchill and Vander Wall, 1990). But for African Americans, the effort to impose Eurocentric gender relations on blacks as the price of entry into the economic mainstream was ultimately the least publicized and most devastating aspect of America's domestic war against its youth and minority rebellions.

The impact of these developments on black women was unprecedented. Essentially, what black women experienced was a profound betrayal by their men and by their communities. Many black women were angered and deeply hurt by this betrayal. As a result, some abandoned community-building and culture-bearing roles. Their abdication was both a response to individual rejection and a search for a new collective gender identity.

VII

In the 1960s and 1970s, black women's leadership was systematically attacked and dismantled. Black women's collective response to this attack was to stop organizing a political infrastructure that assumed a connection between gender consciousness and the continued viability of African American community. Black women virtually stopped mobilizing against sexual violence, homophobia, and misogyny in society in general and in the black community in particular. In short, black intellectuals and leaders neutralized gender as a force for social change (James, 1996). The impact on the black community was devastating.

As the crisis unfolded, community building became increasingly problematic because of unresolved gender conflicts. For example, some black feminists argued that acceptance of traditional roles of culture bearing and community building strengthened black patriarchy and diminished black women's struggle for acceptance in black leadership roles. In their view, any acceptance of past traditions would perpetuate black gender inequality. Others began to argue that black women artists should be free to exempt themselves from community caretaking to maintain their focus on intellectual production. In addition, some black feminists disparaged community building by arguing that taking responsibility for black communities replicated capitalism and perpetuated inherently misogynist and homophobic forms of social organization.

These criticisms of community building assume that caretaking roles are intrinsically repressive and therefore rob black women of their freedom and agency. There are countless black women activists, however, whose experience confirms in two ways that just the opposite is true. First, there are many ways to strengthen culture and to nurture communities that are progressive and liberating. Second, the integrity of black artistic and intellectual production (i.e., how political, social, cultural, or economic concerns affect blacks) demands a sustained connection to black people as well as the isolation required to produce works of value. Clearly, these views close the debate about the meaning of community and the importance of black culture.

Black women's search for gender identity in America will always entail a search for what being a black woman means to family, community, race, and country. If black women do not take responsibility for maintaining a cultural tradition of political activism, it will be because they cannot define their political self-interest in terms larger than their individual or gender-group needs. If black women continue to eschew organized responses to black misogyny and homophobia, they will continue to cultivate a diminished sense of their capacity as women to change their lives or to have a positive impact on the lives of their families or their communities. In other words, the crisis will continue.

VIII

Despite the social and political conflicts raging around black gender identity, black feminism often romanticized the historical contributions of black womanhood without directly addressing the women whom these conflicts left powerless, ashamed, and angry. Without organized support to address these concerns, some black women began to engage in faulty strategies to cope with their sense of disappointment and isolation.

In my view, black feminists did not write about this crisis as it was felt or experienced because they connected their analyses of sex, gender, and class oppression to internecine debates within second-wave feminism rather than to what was actually happening to black women. On the one hand, black feminists were busy fighting racism within the feminist movement itself; on the other hand, they were also trying to defend themselves against charges of betrayal leveled by both male and female black nationalists.[1] These power struggles led to politically correct depictions of black women that stressed uncompromising integrity and passionate commitment to the cause of black people. Black feminism as a protest movement was not prepared to acknowledge that after 1965, the political and cultural climate in America turned our legacy against us. During this period, black women's proud standard of womanhood was increasingly depicted as the root cause of black pathology. As our traditional identity was rejected, black women became immobilized and moved away from the development of their political culture.

Although black women are enormously resilient and many are very successful, their political and economic power remains fragmented and ineffective. The social message they receive about their role in society stresses individual achievement but often fails to promote collective responsibility for the welfare of youth and the rebirth of community among African Americans. Even when black women are encouraged to get involved in their local communities, their involvement is promoted in an apolitical context. The importance of rebuilding black women's political culture is rarely discussed. Promoting volunteerism such as mentoring or building homes in local communities, efforts spearheaded by such notables as Colin Powell or Oprah Winfrey, is noteworthy and desirable. However, a commitment to build homes for needy families should include, for example, both political education and political action, given that in 1996 nationwide, 15 million families were impoverished enough to qualify for housing subsidies, yet federal funding allowed only 4.5 million families to receive such assistance.[2]

Mobilizing around quality-of-life issues such as housing, education, child care, jobs, and economic disinvestment involves understanding the interdependence of gender, race, and class as well as appreciating the impact of public policy on local communities. When the political socialization of black women involves teaching ourselves to make these connections, the crisis will end. Moreover, if black women want to end the crisis of belief and the malaise affecting the growth and development of their political culture, they must first promote their own health and healing. The pathway to such health and healing lies in strengthening our connections to each other and rebuilding black communities as places of nurture and transcendence. This will require us to adapt our historical standards of black womanhood to fit our present circumstances. For example, black women will need to pay more attention to the process of teaching black girls to pursue their individual aspirations as well as their collective self-interest. Young black girls need encouragement to join in creating a shared vision for their communities and in organizing collective efforts to achieve that vision. As they plan and do the work of making communities better places in which to live, they will learn that they are responsible for their own lives and for the preservation of their culture.

With broader support from black communities, black youths can learn to use the emotional and spiritual tools inherent in our cultural legacy to meet their needs for protection and fulfillment. In this way, black youths and young adults can reverse patterns that adversely influence their peer relationships, their choice of sexual partners, and/or their relationships with their own children.

IX

Dealing with the effects of the crisis of black womanhood will be difficult for several reasons. Individual black women differ sharply over what issues can best be addressed by mobilizing politically. Moreover, black women may have deeply held political beliefs about a particular set of issues but may not have access to networks that could give legitimate political expression to those beliefs. Furthermore, black women's marginal economic status, family responsibilities, and tenuous institutional power reduce access to and opportunities for their sustained political activity. In addition, the reasons for limiting political activity vary across class hierarchies. For example, middle-class black women who were active in the 1960s and 1970s may believe that their earlier contributions justify their present lack of political involvement. Low-income women often express anger at the seemingly endless betrayals by black middle-class leadership and at the failures of public policy to address their survival concerns. Feminist coalitions and labor unions compete to address the concerns of black women workers sometimes without realizing that their needs as workers are inextricably linked to their needs as mothers, providers, community members, and so on. Corporate hostility to unionism as well as narrowly focused and competing union-organizing strategies are probably more responsible for the problems in organizing black women workers than are complacency, anger, nihilism, or social pathology.

It would be a mistake to argue that black women are not deeply concerned about their quality of life and about the lives of their families. Concerns for race solidarity, community, quality education, health care, and economic justice find both episodic and long-term expression, from block clubs to legislative campaigns. Nonetheless, black women's political behavior has been affected by the denigration of their role as culture bearers and community builders. Black women are organizing, but they have yet to develop the sustained political infrastructure that could give full expression to their political agency.

National black advocacy groups still struggle to build and maintain viable local policy and advocacy networks. Too often, however, these groups are connected to prominent black leaders rather than to solid grassroots organizations. Church-based groups and sororities provide a strong organizing base but are not always successful in mobilizing women from all income levels. Moreover, these organizations do not consistently address the issues of power and privilege that divide black women from each other.

Despite these challenges, black women are responsible for solving the crisis of black womanhood and for healing themselves. As we transform our traditions into new strategies for survival and transcendence, we will create viable solutions to this crisis. Through political action, black women can uphold traditional standards of black womanhood and explore new cultural sources of self-knowledge. We need to recognize that building physical and emotional spaces among black people is essential for our development as women and for the continued progress of our people. After all, the physical locations of black communities are rich sources of history and heritage. This is as true of black neighborhoods in decline as it is of communities chosen by more affluent blacks.

Although the specific configuration of community may change, the idea of community means people sharing common interests and connecting to a common history. Rebuilding the unique political culture of black women is necessary for the development of individual black Americans and for the continued contributions of black people to the broader society.

5. The Economic Context of Black Women's Activism

Ghetto inhabitants make up less than 10 percent of people living in poverty. By contrast, about half of the adult poor work. These people are poor not because they are unable or unwilling to work. They are poor because they work at jobs that do not pay. Poverty is a business issue then because most poor people are part of the current or future US work force.

—**Mary Jo Bane and David T. Ellwood, "Is American Business Working for the Poor?"**

Besides the loss of political culture, black women have economic concerns that inhibit their political activism. Feminists have not paid sufficient attention to black economic decline. It should therefore be stated at the outset that the social consequences of economic issues such as the flight of capital from the inner city, the changing nature of work, and U.S. trade policy are women's issues. Although black and brown feminists have consistently focused on issues of race and class for the most part, they have used social rather than economic frameworks to structure their analyses. Thus, feminist commentary often discusses the effects of poverty without clearly analyzing the forces that cause it. Feminist political analysis rarely connects women's lives to economic policy debates such as global trade policy, industrial policy, the impact of technology on world economies, or the need for more resources to enhance local economic development. Feminists have taken positions on domestic policy issues such as health care, child care, welfare reform, family leave, and small-business development, but their recommendations often have limited impact on local, regional, or national economic policy. If feminists continue to retreat from strong economic advocacy, American economic policy makers will continue to assume that the United States and other capital markets around the world have the right to exploit the labor of women and children through low wages and poor working conditions.

I

The legacy of supply-side economics in a global economy is now known. For example, the U.S. Census Bureau reports that from 1989 to 1993, the typical American household lost 7 percent of its annual income; and from 1992 to 1993, more than one million new people fell into poverty. In 1994, despite the overall growth of the U.S. economy, more than one third of American households still saw their income decline. Social economist Bennett Harrison provides a broad analysis of the problem at hand:

> The average post W.W. II earnings [in terms of rate of growth of earn-
> ings] peaked in the early 1970s. [Today] wage inequality [is] grow-
> ing...even as the economy has expanded, in contradiction to all previ-
> ous evidence and to the predictions of standard theory.... The proportion
> of Americans earning poverty-level wages [has increased] among men
> and by some accounts among women. (1994, 192)

In his essay "The Parable of the Talents," Henry Louis Gates Jr. states the problem for black Americans:

> What makes all of this of particular concern is the swelling ranks of
> the black poor, a category that (like the black middle class) now en-
> compasses about a third of black families. More than half of all black
> males between twenty-five and thirty-four are jobless or "underem-
> ployed." (Gates and West, 1997, 24)

By 1996, the Clinton administration was touting a robust economy and the dismantling of Reagan-Bush economics. Clinton claimed credit for raising the minimum wage, reducing the federal deficit, lowering unemployment, fostering a new era of job growth, and keeping inflationary pressures at bay. Indeed, Clinton economic policies were bolstered by declines in the poverty rate between 1996 and 1997. By 1997, both the number and percentage of families in poverty had declined. For example, the number of poor blacks dropped from 9.7 million in 1996 to 9.1 million in 1997. In that same year, the poverty rate for black families dropped from 26.1 percent to 23.6 percent. This was good news. In 1998, the overall black poverty rate of 26.1 percent was the lowest rate since 1959, yet the rate was significantly higher than the white, non-Hispanic rate of 8.6 percent and only slightly lower than the Hispanic rate of 27.1 percent (Dalaker and Naifeh, 1998).[1]

Despite these declines, most American households need two working family members to make ends meet, job security is a major concern, and more than forty million Americans have no health insurance, a higher number than when Clinton first took office in 1992. Moreover, America continues to shed its highly skilled industrial and manufacturing workforce. For example, the Bureau of Labor Statistics reported 1,336 mass layoffs by employers in November 1999. (A mass layoff is defined as a layoff involving at least fifty persons from a single firm.) The number of workers involved was 139,508. Manufacturing industries accounted for more than 25 percent of these mass layoffs. In a report discussing what policies states should pursue to remain competitive in the global economy, the National Governors' Association stated that "in the new economy, new jobs and businesses are being born while almost as many jobs are dying."[2]

Although unemployment rates continue to decline, many people seeking full-time employment are working in temporary jobs without benefits. In 1995, the contingent workforce, or those in temporary jobs, was at an all-time high. Moreover, the economy continues to produce a significant number of jobs that cannot support families. For example, the Illinois Occupational Information Coordinating Council reported that in Illinois in the 1990s, more than 40 percent of new jobs in retail, health, and service industries required little more than a high school diploma and paid a maximum of $1.00 to $2.50 above the minimum wage.[3]

Given these structural changes in the world economy, the economic policies that progressive women can support begin from the standpoint of developing a U.S. economy that minimizes downward shifts in the economic well-being of its citizens. Providing better wages and income supports for people desperately trying to move up the economic ladder is as important as the current focus on increased worker productivity, new product development, and the expansion of global trade. By 1997, despite the growth in earnings, low unemployment, and declining poverty rates, low- and moderate-income Americans, workers in industries hurt by foreign competition, and workers with little formal education were clearly among those whom prosperity was leaving behind.

If mainstream feminism can be criticized for not effectively challenging U.S. economic policy, black women have had even less of an impact on such policies, despite their greater willingness to advance economic concerns. Black feminists have often failed politically to challenge current notions of economic growth based on free trade, the benefits of global integration, and the assumption that technological innovation will automatically raise the standard of living for most Americans. Improving the economic life chances for the millions of women participating in welfare reform, to name one policy, will severely test the limits of policies designed for moderate economic growth. The potential impact of these policies on low- and moderate-income women should drive black feminists to support a domestic economy that promotes both the efficient production of goods and the development of an effective and adequately paid labor force. Unfortunately, too few of us are engaged in the work of building coalitions to voice alternative economic priorities.

Scholars and activists discuss the economic decline of black men but rarely talk about the decline of black women's economic status and its effect on the black community. The decline of black women's activism is also rarely discussed in relation to U.S. economic policy. This is surprising, given that black women are the most disadvantaged segment of the U.S. labor market relative to the annual percentage increase in their earnings and the quality of their jobs. Black women fared especially poorly from the mid-1980s through the early 1990s, as the ravages of unemployment and recession affected every black woman in America either directly or indirectly. To fully assess the impact of a changing economy on black women and their families, researchers are advancing theories of black economic development grounded in the changing conditions of global labor markets (Wilson, 1996). What is needed, however, is a gender analysis of how economic distress affects sexuality and gender identity. A women-centered critique of how U.S. economic policy affects both individual life choices and the public culture of local communities could link prevailing norms regarding male-female relationships to distinct sets of economic policy decisions. Such a critique might ask, for example, how were black women and the black community affected by the fact that African American men in white-collar jobs experienced an overall increase in income from 1979 through 1990 whereas during the same period blue-collar black men, especially young ones, experienced double-digit unemployment? Black men with a college education moved into private-sector employment at a rate faster than any other group in the workforce during the 1980s, but less-educated black men and black women were caught in a downward spiral of employment segregation, income loss, and narrowing opportunity. The effect of economic isolation on the development of black women's sexuality and related gender roles needs systematic exploration.[4]

II

On August 22, 1996, President Clinton signed the Personal Responsibility and Work Opportunity Reconciliation Act. This act eliminated Aid for Families with Dependent Children (AFDC) and created block grants for states to provide time-limited cash assistance to poor families. The act also created the Temporary Assistance for Needy Families program (TANF), which mandates strict work requirements and places new restrictions on child care, food assistance, and income supplementation. Welfare recipients are required to work once they have received assistance under the program for twenty-four months.[5]

This politically engineered version of welfare reform was ostensibly designed to use employment to fix the problem of subsidized social pathology and family dysfunction. Fortunately, some welfare recipients are finding jobs, because welfare reform is occurring during an extended period of unprecedented economic growth. Yet despite the number of politicians and talk-radio hosts who supported the bill, there is little compelling evidence that these reform measures will reduce poverty, cut welfare dependence, save taxpayers' money, and move families toward the economic mainstream.[6] In fact, it is just as likely that in some states, the current reforms will inflict unprecedented pain and hardship on families that have already experienced generations of poverty. Because the welfare-reform strategy provides financial incentives for states to restrict welfare eligibility, to lower caseloads through sanctions, to impose work requirements and family caps, and to move poor women from welfare to low-wage work, it may eventually plunge more families into poverty. This could occur even as some women benefit from job opportunities.

Real welfare reform deserves our support. Genuine reform, however, should be designed to lift women out of poverty, not simply to cut the welfare rolls. It is possible that during periods of economic decline, the current reforms will require states to reduce already limited benefits or to violate work-participation mandates and lose federal dollars.

In addition to welfare reform, the economic circumstances of black life confirm that black social decline is characterized by forms of community dysfunction and social pathology that are strongly associated with poverty. An analysis of the scope and severity of problems related to poverty, therefore, should undergird a feminist analysis of U.S. economic policy. A focus on poverty, its impact on women, and its consequences for all Americans is consistent with the gender realities of these issues. Areas for analysis include the following:[7]

- *Persistent poverty.* Although most poor people are white, blacks bear a disproportionate share of poverty. The U.S. Census Bureau reported that in 1999, the black, non-Hispanic population in the United States was 35.078 million. In 1999, blacks made up 12.8 percent of the population and 23.6 percent of all families below the poverty rate, whereas 8.4 percent of those families were white. About one in four white female-headed households lived below poverty in 1997, whereas black female-headed households accounted for 39.8 percent of families below poverty.

- *Income disparity.* As reported by the U.S. Census Bureau, the median income of black families in 1996 was $26,520, compared to $47,023 for white families. Twenty-three percent of black families earned $50,000 or more, whereas 18 percent of black families earned less than $10,000 per year and 28 percent earned between $10,000 and $24,999. In 1996, less than 20 percent of black women earned $35,000 or more. The median earnings of black women were $21,470, whereas the median earnings of black men were $26,400.

- *Inadequate health care.* In the United States, advocates estimate that the number of people with HIV ranges from 650,000 to 900,000. The Centers for Disease Control and Prevention reported that in 1997, an estimated 49,689 people were diagnosed with AIDS. Blacks make up 12.1 percent of the population but more than 28 percent of all AIDS cases and more than 47 percent of all new cases of AIDS. The rate of HIV infection increased steadily among blacks between 1980 and 1988. During this period, the AIDS death rate for black women rose from 4.4 percent to 10.3 percent per 100,000. The Centers for Disease Control and Prevention report that black women make up more than 50 percent of all women with AIDS. Nationwide, despite a decrease in newly reported cases, AIDS is among the leading causes of death among African Americans between the ages of twenty-five and forty-four. It is the third leading cause of death among black women aged fifteen to forty-four, and a black woman in that age group is nine times more likely to die of AIDS than a white woman.

- *Inadequate educational preparation.* An estimated 42 million Americans are functionally illiterate. It is estimated that each year more than 800,000 young people leave high school before graduation. More than 40 percent of these youths are African American.

- *The growing threat of violence.* Although overall the United States has experienced a decrease in crime over the last several years, public health statistics indicate that homicide is one of the leading causes of death among black men and black women between the ages of twenty-five and thirty-four. One of the most disturbing trends is that homicide is the major cause of preventable deaths among African American adolescent males. In 1991, college campuses reported a 40 percent increase in racial or hate violence over the previous year.

- *Job growth and unemployment.* In May 1999, the black male unemployment rate was 7.8 percent. During the same period, the black female unemployment rate was 7.2 percent. This compares with a 3.2 percent unemployment rate for white males and females. Nearly 47 percent of all employed black males aged sixteen or over were employed as laborers, operators, fabricators, or service workers. Thirty-seven percent of all employed black women held the same occupations. Job growth was lowering unemployment, but there was significant regional variation in the availability of employment. For example, in September 1998, the national unemployment rate was 4.6 percent. The Midwest unemployment rate, however, ranged from 2.0 percent in Bloomington-Normal, Illinois, to 6.4 percent in Kankakee, Illinois.

Where are the jobs? What types of jobs are we creating? Who will get these jobs? How can those who work at low-income jobs still have an adequate standard of living? These are among the central questions of our time. The reality of poverty is that in one-half to three-fourths of all poor families, at least one adult works and most of the rest look for work, at least periodically. Most of the members of the nonprofessional temporary labor force are women who have no health or pension benefits. Slow wage growth, regressive tax policies, the high cost of child care, the escalating cost of health care, the decline of affordable housing, inadequate educational preparation, and increased competition for America's most desirable jobs continue to limit poor people's access to economic opportunity.

III

Since the 1980s, a number of high-profile studies have documented how poverty and discrimination have resulted in wide economic disparities between whites and blacks and among middle- and lower-income blacks. For example, in 1989, the National Research Council published a study entitled *A Common Destiny: Blacks and American Society.* This report discussed the growing income gap between the black middle class and the black poor. The report states:

> During the 1960s incomes were growing for most black (and white) families. Blacks in all income ranges gained relative to their counterparts (in real income). In fact, as the rate of poverty declined, the relative gains were greatest for black families with the lowest incomes.... Then during the 1970s reductions in poverty rates slowed leaving approximately one-third of black families with incomes below poverty throughout the decade and into the 1980s. (Jaynes and Williams, 1989, 279)

This study found that differences in black individual and family income relative to that of whites were largely a consequence of labor-market discrimination. Differential treatment of young black males competing for jobs, as well as instances of employment dislocation, resulted in a corresponding increase in female-headed families. Marian Wright Edelman argues this point in her book *Families in Peril: An Agenda for Social Change*:

> There is more than a correlation between declining black male employment and declining marriage rates among young blacks.... When a pregnant single woman is resolved to bear the child, marriage is most likely under active consideration. If the father of the child, presumably a few years older than herself, is potentially a good provider, marriage may well result. But if the proportion of young males who are potentially good providers falls, we would expect to see the prenatal marriage rate decline.... My basic conclusion is that the key to bolstering black families, alleviating the growth in female-headed households, and reducing black child poverty lies in improved education, training, and employment opportunities for black males and females. (1987, 14)

The 1998 edition of the National Urban League's *The State of Black America* reports that nearly two-thirds of all black households had zero or negative net financial assets. The extensive data and sound analysis produced by these and other studies provide compelling evidence of the failure of Reagan-Bush economic policies to improve the quality of life for black people and, as it turns out, for almost everybody else as well. In fact, Kevin Phillips's study *The Politics of Rich and Poor* argues that the enormous concentration of wealth in the United States that resulted from Reagan-Bush economic policies has created an opportunity for the emergence of a new political consensus driven by the frustrations of the 95 percent of Americans who saw their incomes stagnate or fall during the 1980s (1990, 16–17).

So far, Phillips has been wrong. Despite compelling evidence that relatively few American households benefited from the Reagan-Bush response to the globalization of the economy, Americans have been more focused on cutting income subsidies for the poor than on cutting subsidies and entitlements for those who use government contacts, influence, and subsidies to enhance shareholder value or private wealth. In the mid- to late 1990s, President Bill Clinton and the Republican factions that dominated both houses of Congress and a majority of state legislatures had a limited amount of political capital, and they were not about to spend it on issues of economic justice. As a result, neither the poor nor members of the middle class fully understood the necessary trade-offs involved in promoting moderate but steady economic growth while sacrificing jobs and wages for profits. During the Reagan-Bush years, few of us realized that while organized political constituencies were fighting to tighten benefit requirements for social services, job training, and public assistance, the top 20 percent of American households earned 48.2 percent of all available income, whereas the bottom 20 percent of American households earned just 3.6 percent of available income (Phillips, 1990, 28).

The economic policies of Clinton's second term assiduously avoided economic-stimulus packages in favor of new free-trade deals, a modest increase in the minimum wage, and private-sector incentives to hire the welfare population. In addition, the president proposed to expand Medicare, invest in education, expand the earned-income tax credit, and save Social Security. These initiatives were more or less popular with Clinton's political base. Yet the nation lacks a bold strategy to align current workforce preparation policies with the needs of those whom the labor market has failed. Fundamental to this discussion is the question of whether the economy can continue to produce enough livable-wage jobs for all who need them. Even if there are enough jobs, the global competitiveness of the labor force means that many workers, including those with few marketable skills, will suffer bouts of unemployment and economic instability. To remain competitive, these workers will need local, regional, and national governments to help them prepare for new jobs and maintain an adequate standard of living while they adapt to the needs of a rapidly changing economy. These issues are critical for American workers, especially for those who seem destined to trade welfare subsistence for wage subsistence.

What often gets lost in debates about how the poor can participate in the mainstream economy is the fact that although poor people have many social problems, most are capable of responding to opportunity if it offers a real chance to increase their income and their stake in the fabric of the general society. Programs that invest in the capabilities of the American workforce and ensure a reasonable standard of living have simply not held a serious place on anyone's political agenda. Few leaders on the horizon possess both the vision and the political skill necessary to connect the long-term interests of the poor, working poor, and working classes with the economic interests of the beleaguered middle class.[8]

In the Reagan-Bush years, the middle class became more concerned about their tenuous standard of living and were led to blame government's help of the poor for their plight. As Americans better understand the realities of the global economy, they may realize that government economic policy and protected business classes, not welfare queens, are robbing them of their old-age pensions (Mishel and Bernstein, 1994).

IV

A disproportionate number of poor people are black and female. Given this fact, a resurgence of black women's activism should be inevitable. If this is true, then the question of organizing across the income and attitude gaps between the black middle and working classes becomes crucial. Black Americans have divergent class interests, goals, aspirations, and expectations and will need comprehensive strategies, effective tactics, and skillful leadership to form broad coalitions.

A strong feminist economic analysis of the impact of increased globalization on people of the middle class could potentially connect their plight directly to that of the poor and could bolster a constituency powerful enough to demand policies that invest in the American workforce. Education, health, regional economic development, balanced trade policies, and adequate support for family life should be part of the cost of doing business in America. The benefits of improving our workforce should be better products, a better quality of life, and more opportunity for everyone, especially the bottom 20 percent.

Since these economic issues directly affect the future of black women and black families, black women's economic activism could give visibility and voice to millions of poor people whose issues are rarely considered. Without strong economic analysis and sound policy alternatives, black women cannot challenge the basic premises of social and fiscal conservatives. The conservative political agenda places the major focus of national domestic policy on personal responsibility rather than on economic policies that could benefit the poor as well as the majority of American workers.

Poverty theory of the late 1980s and early 1990s effectively blamed government support of the poor for the problem of poverty and connected the lower standard of living for the middle class with the problem of entitlement spending rather than with the problem of corporate mergers, takeovers, layoffs, and tax loopholes. The conservative agenda was premised on the notion that the poor contribute to their own poverty and that therefore government attempts to alleviate poverty through social programs will always fail. The fact that black people's behavior affects their economic well-being is a thesis made explicit in the works of Charles Murray and in the works of black conservatives like Thomas Sowell (1994). For example, in 1984, Murray's *Losing Ground: American Social Policy, 1950–1980* analyzed the rise of inner-city crime, drug abuse, unemployment, and housing decay. He concluded that the rising incidence of social disorganization among the poor was evidence that the social programs of the 1960s had failed. Murray's work, highly influential in forming the Reagan social policy agenda, blamed government social programs for black marital instability, an increase in female heads of household, and the lower labor-force participation rates of black males. His analysis turned the liberal poverty argument on its head by claiming that social dysfunction causes poverty rather than the other way around.

Murray's policy recommendations were aimed at severing the "greedy and undeserving" poor from the "good and worthy" poor using a combination of social-spending cuts, tighter welfare eligibility requirements, low-income tax credits, and deregulation. In the eighties and early nineties, these views created enormous tension within the black community concerning who was to blame for black decline, what to do about it, and who should pay to fix it. In response to this tension, politically conservative members of the new black middle class felt justified in distancing themselves from the plight of the poor.

In contrast to the writings of social conservatives like Charles Murray, Robert Reich's book *The Work of Nations* (1991) presents a clear alternative. Reich argues that in a global economy like ours, the only real national resource that ensures a competitive advantage is people. Reich is part of the first wave of scholars and policy makers who are seeking to create a new economic paradigm built around people. People strategies focus on economic development and include increased attention to human capital, renewed interest in regional economic growth, and government-backed support for the creation of high-performance workplaces. Other strategies being considered to improve wages include microenterprise development, entrepreneurship, direct-wage subsidies, minimum-wage increases, and higher tax credits to help keep people who have low-wage jobs from living in poverty.

Despite some projects in these areas and much discussion about these new approaches, there is still no consensus regarding the government's role in solving the problems of long-term poverty. Even when Americans concede that poor people need a safety net, there is no political consensus on the issue of who will pay for the social programs that Americans agree are necessary. The fact that most politicians are not working to build political consensus to alleviate the effects of poverty speaks volumes about government timidity and ineffectiveness. Global economic competition, unbridled capitalism in emerging markets, and special-interest politics capture America's attention and crowd out any sustained and actionable interest in the nation's poor.

The politics of bipartisanship ensures that there will be no long-term consensus on how or whether the government can help workers maintain an adequate standard of living during times of job loss or economic dislocation. The political climate in the aftermath of President Clinton's impeachment for perjury and obstruction of justice made it impossible for him to get Republican support for the parts of his domestic economic agenda that would have helped low-income and working-class Americans. Although Clinton had been impeached, the overzealousness of socially conservative Republicans ensured that he ultimately strengthened his hold on his office and weakened the unity of both parties going into the 2000 election. Thus, whatever coalition the new president or Congress can put together to pass a fair domestic economic agenda will be tenuous and difficult to maintain.

Despite growing economic prosperity, Republican fiscal conservatives continued to dismantle social programs that provided a safety net for the poor. For example, the 105th Congress, the same Congress that impeached Clinton, passed the Omnibus Appropriations Bill for Fiscal 1999, a $520 billion budget package. In this budget, federal aid to state and local governments increased by $28 billion, and all block grants received funding increases except the Title XX Social Services Block Grant (SSBG). This program, which provides a range of services for low-income families and individuals within each state, including child care and after-school programs, was cut by $390 million. In addition, the Transportation Equity Act cut more funding for the SSBG beginning in fiscal year 2001 and reduced the ability of state governments to maintain existing services by transferring Temporary Assistance for Needy Families (TANF) funds to the SSBG.[9]

American voters worship prosperity, and fiscal conservatives stand ready to convince them that the nation cannot cut taxes, reduce the national debt, save Social Security, and provide social services for the poor at the same time. Yet even modest cuts in social services hurt poor people and their children. Black women need to advocate for an adequate safety net for Americans who need it. Black women are politically sophisticated enough to initiate a broad-based economic development campaign in local communities. Such a campaign could mobilize the poor and the middle class around sound economic policies that support people and not just corporate profits.

The analysis of economic change and its affect on issues of family, class, and community should be linked to political action that supports a new alignment of industrial, economic, education, and labor policies. This alignment could effectively guarantee that those who have been traditionally excluded from the economic mainstream have the opportunity to compete in the new economy.

V

The capacity of feminist theory to analyze social problems and to stimulate collective action on behalf of the best solutions to those problems is crucial to building a constituency that is antipoverty, antiracist, pro-woman, and pro-community. If there is to be a new movement against poverty and all forms of class injustice, its natural constituency is women. Women and their children have a great deal at stake. Black feminists should develop women-centered models that examine the effects of black economic underdevelopment worldwide. We live in the long shadow of an upward redistribution of wealth that continues to be fueled by the global movement of capital and by laissez-faire economic policies. Black women know that it is in their collective interest to demand economic solutions that have the potential to include the poor as part of the economic mainstream. Authentic feminist social action, organizing, and leadership development should thus emerge as the logical outcome of feminist economic analysis.

Feminists need to conceptualize and negotiate women's economic interests more broadly and with the full realization that market economies are woefully inadequate when it comes to providing for the needs of people. As we Americans contemplate changes in economic policy, we must clearly understand that only a comprehensive, full-scale strategy with targeted interventions designed largely by local communities and paid for by public and private investment will measurably improve the life chances for all of us, including low-income people. Unless as a nation we invest consistently in quality health care, child care, affordable housing, education, a broad range of social services, and effective job training, American competitiveness will suffer. America needs its public and private sectors to work together to pursue economic objectives that include helping people escape poverty. Whether we do this or not is a matter of economic policy, and economic policy decisions are ultimately political. Robert Heilbroner and Lester Thurow make a similar point in their book *Economics Explained*:

> The real challenge does not lie in our economic problems, but in the political and moral values that always enter into our economic determinations. Economics is the language we use to talk about the workings and options of our system, but it is not the language ... [we use] to appraise the value of the system or decide what elements to preserve

or change. Politics and morality — our collective wills and our private value systems — remain the bedrock of society. The outcome of the crisis of our times will reflect the strength of that will and the quality of those values. (1994, 260)

In the era of globalization and information, black people cannot afford to be complacent or confused. They have been ill served by the discredited and timid liberalism of the 1960s and by the economic Darwinism of the 1980s and 1990s. Feminist theorizing must include nonnegotiable demands for social and economic justice. These demands should be uppermost in the minds of black feminists seeking to rebuild their communities.

6. The Particulars of Un-Negation

In what public discourse does the reference to black people not exist? It exists in every one of this nation's mightiest struggles. The presence of black people is not only a major referent in the framing of the Constitution, it is also in the battle over enfranchising unpropertied citizens, women, the illiterate. It is there in the construction of a free and public school system . . . and legal definitions of justice. . . . The presence of black people is inherent, along with gender and family ties, in the earliest lesson every child is taught regarding his or her distinctiveness. Africanism is inextricable from the definition of Americanness — from its origins on through its integrated or disintegrating twentieth-century self.

    —Toni Morrison, *Playing in the Dark: Whiteness and the Literary Imagination*

Although the role of insurgent intellectual suits my temperament, I'm really not all doom and gloom. One source of my optimism stems from the resilience of the human spirit. Another stems from the remarkable creativity of black people. I'm especially fascinated by how creative thinking and artistic production respond to the dynamics of race, gender, class, culture, and community. In the early 1990s, Michele Wallace wrote a widely published essay, "Variations on Negation and the Heresy of Black Feminist Creativity," which crystallized the dilemmas of black feminist intellectuals. Since the publication of this essay, black intellectuals have been discovered by the broader community, and their overall role in contemporary society continues to be defined through such works as Joy James's *Transcending the Talented Tenth,* Alice Walker's *The Same River Twice,* bell hooks and Cornel West's *Breaking Bread,* Beverly Guy-Sheftall's *Words of Fire,* Carole Boyce Davies's *Black Women, Writing, and Identity,* and Patricia Hill Collins's *Fighting Words.* Wallace's essay, however, is among the first works to identify key issues involved in creating black feminist discourse. It is also among the first to focus on the connection between community and black women's creativity. As such, the essay contains fundamental insights and raises significant concerns about black women's creativity, community, and struggle for a just society.

I

Both versions of "Variations on Negation and the Heresy of Black Feminist Creativity"—one published in Henry Louis Gates Jr.'s *Reading Black, Reading Feminist* and the other in Michele Wallace's book *Invisibility Blues*—make compelling yet disconcerting statements about the creativity of black women.[1] Wallace's main premise is that black women are systematically denied access to channels for the production of intellectual discourse and creativity. She argues that black women's experiences are structured by the dominant culture in ways that place those experiences and their wisdom outside of the language, history, and tradition of critical discourse. As a result, Wallace argues, there is a radical disconnection between what black women create and what society considers to be knowledge.

This argument and Wallace's assertion that black women's creative expression springs from a desire "to make the world a place that will be safe for women of color, their men, and their children" (216) raise important questions regarding the role of black feminists in contemporary culture. For example, are black women (whether they call themselves feminists or not) using their creativity to make the world safer? Given that Wallace defines the goal of black feminist creative production as political transformation for black people as a group, several questions are more to the point: Are black feminist intellectuals and activists assuming leadership in the long march toward a better world? Are we challenging cultural hegemony, or, having made a small but important niche for ourselves, are we the minimally/minimal established/establishment? Are we the outlaw renegades and truth tellers of public discourse, or are we simply the predictable minority report?

Wallace observes that the intellectual production of black feminists has not successfully challenged what she calls the "exclusionary parlor games of canon formation and the production of knowledge" (214). Her essay contends that the cultural elite and black feminists themselves are responsible for the lack of theoretical analysis by black women, because each group has deemed black women incapable of such production: "To the extent that art exists as a by-product of diverse acts of interpretation and analysis, black feminist creativity is virtually non-existent." She continues: "Prevented from assuming a commensurable role in critical theory and production of knowledge by a combination of external and internal pressures—economic and psychological—[black feminist creativity] is confined to the aesthetic and the commercial" (218). Intellectuals, Wallace claims, assume that "black women have no interest in criticism, interpretation, and theoretical analysis—no capacity for it" (214).

Although black feminists such as Patricia Hill Collins, Paula Giddings, Darlene Clark Hine, Hortense Spillers, Angela Davis, and bell hooks, among others, have produced significant theory and social criticism since Wallace's essay first appeared, she raises a still-legitimate concern about the role of black feminist creativity in the struggle for social justice. As Wallace describes the many ways that black women are negated by the intellectual and cultural elite, she exposes the structural reasons why most black feminist intellectuals remain virtually unknown outside their fields. In addition to black feminists' exclusion from mainstream exposure, Wallace perceives their lack of theoretical production as a consequence of black women's relationship to the feminist movement as a whole: "At the same time the 'other' of the 'other' is resistant to theoretical articulation—hence the black feminist fear of theory.... [As a result,] black feminist interpretation [is] radically nonexistent, or invisible, in the realm of dominant discourse" (228).

Wallace's use of the term *negation* connotes negation in the dialectical sense. Wallace, however, is not using negation to theorize the opposite of capitalist class relations in order to sustain revolutionary thinking. She is not engaged in a "negation of the negation" or a critique of "all that is" in the sense that Raya Dunayevskaya meant when she used the term in her theorizing of Marxist humanism, *Women's Liberation and the Dialectics of Revolution* (1996). Wallace is not referring to what Dunayevskaya specifies as the first negation, the overthrow of the capitalist class, or the second negation, the creation of entirely revolutionary social relations. Wallace is simply advancing the not-so-revolutionary notion that black women have not been afforded enough opportunities for intellectual self-expression. She observes that, with too few exceptions, the success of black women writers has been in fields dominated by expressive rather than analytical discourse. For her, this suggests a cultural conspiracy to relegate black women writers to roles that white readers are comfortable with. Wallace asserts that as a result, much of black feminist discourse is simply not allowed to be relevant to black women.

Despite the fact that Wallace is right about the limits imposed on black women's creativity, her explanation for the lack of black feminist interpretation of life and culture in mainstream discourse is too predictable. For Wallace, all of these concerns fall under the category of negation. Her comments regarding the multiple variations of black female negation are valid, but her approach is thoroughly anticipated and is therefore neither revolutionary nor new. Wallace merely expropriates revolutionary language to protest black feminist exclusion from the dominant mainstream: "Another way of describing variations on negation would be to call them negative images, although I prefer 'variations on negation' because negation seems indispensable to a dialectical critical process. . . . Variations on negation confront . . . the radical being and non-being of women of color" (228).

"Variations on Negation" issues the classic Wallace demand for a feminist context that does not negate black women. But as much as I admire this essay, it misrepresents several issues regarding black feminism and feminist creativity. For example, Wallace's explanation of why black feminist theoretical production has been so spotty is replete with standard victimization discourse. She barely mentions that black feminist theoretical invisibility has something to do with black feminists' confusion over whom they create for and why. In other words, our negation is attributable in part to confusion over both our role as black feminists and our motives for creating analytical discourse. Furthermore, Wallace misses a major opportunity to note that our contributions as black feminists will always fall short of achieving broad recognition and new insight if we allow ourselves to create only from a premise of negation.

Finally, Wallace does not acknowledge that the primary thrust of our creativity should be to engage our intellect in ways that give direction to the changing circumstances of black women's lives. Undue concern over the demands of academia or of other members of the intellectual elite fosters a reactive black feminist discourse that ultimately alienates us from the wellspring of our creative expression and from most black women. Unfortunately, Wallace's focus on our erasure obscures our obligation to listen to our people, to affirm their power, and to create a black female discourse that speaks truthfully of who we really are and what that identity means to us and to our history.

II

To better illustrate her use of the concept of negation, Wallace analyzes Houston Baker's work as a backdrop for her discussion of literary criticism and black feminist creativity. In her critique of Baker's *Blues, Ideology, and Afro-American Literature* (1984), Wallace discusses Baker's essay on Richard Wright as illustrative of the problem of black feminist negation:

> Baker's key trope in describing the literature of Richard Wright is a black hole, an area of space in which gravitation is so intense that no light can escape so that it appears absolutely black. Contrary to everything we've been taught to expect of black holes in general, black holes

in space are full, not empty. They are . . . dense stars . . . surrounded by . . . a membrane that prevents the unaltered escape of anything which passes through. . . . Light shining into a black hole disappears. (Wallace, 1990, 217)[2]

For Baker, Richard Wright's work illustrates a black hole/whole. In its depiction of black life, Wright's work is satisfying and complete.

Although the intent of Baker's essay is to challenge the cultural hegemony of whiteness in the pantheon of American literature, Wallace is concerned that as Baker supports his claim that Wright is the undisputed master of black cultural studies, he elevates Wright at the expense of black women writers: "While [Baker] seeming[ly] throws off the mantle of white male cultural hegemony . . . [his claims for Wright] only serve to mask [the] domination and erasure of black feminist or female contributions to the field" (218). Wallace goes on to argue that the products of creative feminists have disappeared into the dense star of blackness that she describes as a niche created by the intellectual elite to erase our cultural production, a place where our creative lights are absorbed and therefore can't shine: "In other words, the black hole represents the dense accumulation, without explanation or inventory, of black feminist creativity" (218).

It is disappointing that Wallace's focus on variations of negation leads her to concentrate on the compressed mass and disappearing lights of black feminist creativity. Because of this focus, she misses a more liberating possibility that she herself uncovers. She writes:

A feminist student who is a physics major at the University of Oklahoma told me something else about black holes when I told her what Baker had said. Physicists now believe black holes may give access to other dimensions. An object or energy enters the black hole, and is infinitely compressed to zero volume. . . . Then it passes through to another dimension, whereupon the object or energy reassumes volume, mass, form, direction, velocity, all the properties of visibility and concreteness. (218)

This suggests that genuine black feminist (or female) artists and intellectuals succumb to the gravitational pull of a star so dense that not even light can escape its gravity. These artists risk alteration or erasure because they are driven by the possibility of exploring new dimensions of human connection beyond what we now know. In other words, as Wallace focuses on negation, she ignores the central paradox at the heart of black feminist creativity and the motivation that compels this creativity in the face of overwhelming odds. When viewed in this context, the same black-hole analogy that Wallace uses as a metaphor for the marginalized creativity of black women can be used to create an alternative framework for black feminist writers of analytical discourse. This framework challenges all black women to garner their creative energies and compress them in order to take a *Star Trek Deep Space Nine* journey through the "worm hole" to explore new dimensions. In short, the real basis of black feminist creativity, whether commercial, analytical, or artistic, is its potential to explore new dimensions — a potential that I believe can be realized only when black feminist creativity is connected to real black people engaged in necessary struggle. I call these risky, scary, spectacular journeys of intellectual flight "particulars of un-negation."

For me, Wallace's use of the black-hole analogy is too focused on the disappearing aspects of black women's creativity. Rather than focusing on how the intellectual elite conspire not to see us — a trope on the variations of negation — it is more interesting to focus on the infinite variations of who we are and what we can become — the particulars of un-negation. By using this phrase, I mean to convey the idea that just as negation exists, so it can also change; it can evolve into its opposite. Just as negation exists, so does un-negation. Un-negation exists and can thus evolve. Both exist simultaneously and are always evolving.

The carefully articulated wisdom and truth of "Variations on Negation" is unsettlingly compromised by its preoccupation with how we are erased or negated by white folks. In the final analysis, the concept of negation draws creative energy away from what we ought to be doing as black feminist intellectuals to speak to and be seen as part of the hopes, dreams, aspirations, needs, and contributions of black people to American culture. Although the fact of negation is undeniable, the focus on negation confuses our agenda. The promise of un-negation lies in its conceptual capacity to validate our work in its own context. The process of un-negation clarifies our job as writers and thinkers, forcing us to find ways to connect to our people and to write and think about what really matters to them. Given this context, our struggle with coded language and virtual annihilation is paradoxically the wellspring of our creativity. Anyone who cares to may listen to us, but when we are constantly speaking to the entrenched and reactionary intellectual marketplace, we feel used, tokenized, or erased. Creating paradigms, languages, and opportunities to utter our own truth about black lives in the powerful shadow of white self-idolatry is the most profound particular of un-negation.

The struggle against sexism, homophobia, and macho challenges black feminists to move beyond the search for recognition by the male intellectual establishment or the feminist elite. A black feminist is called to create a particular and politically useful analysis of black gender oppression. Such analyses honestly plunge us directly into the black holes of race and gender prejudice to find the voices within us and to explore the dimensions of a world often palpably hostile to black collective life. Black feminists are called upon to balance the pursuit of intellectual careers with the responsibility to draw from and to give back to the power base within the black community. In this context, black feminism is a choice about the operation of black gender consciousness. This choice requires us to move beyond the politics of both the academy and the elite to touch the hearts of ordinary black women's experience. When this happens, black feminist theorizing can explain and address the loss of black cultural agency and can embrace new sources of cultural power. Thus, a viable black feminism must acknowledge everyday women/people as the source of our creativity and must challenge everyday black women/people to explore the territory between gender oppression and the dismantling of black cultural agency.

As we begin the twenty-first century, the diminution of black cultural power represents a form of genocide that connects directly to the loss of black women's traditional status as change agents in the community. Replacing this loss of cultural power with the influence of individual black female celebrities, politicians, entertainers, athletes, entrepreneurs, activists, feminists, and intellectuals matters little to ordinary black women, too many of whom are immobilized. It's time for black feminists to see, feel, and use black female agency to reconnect our culture to our community.

The fate of beleaguered black communities, the condition of the economically disadvantaged, and the ultimate survival of black people depend, in part, on constructing a black feminist analytical discourse that links black feminist values to effective social action. Black feminist cultural production must place its truths, its needs, its messages, its modes of discourse, and its unique forms of inquiry at the center of its creativity. It is precisely the black feminist search for a safer world that pulls us into the black hole of potential negation and propels us toward new dimensions of human connectedness through women-centered intellectual activity, cultural commentary, and political activism. These are all viable strategies for black gender empowerment. If, as Wallace states, "there exists no critical discourse, . . . no language specifically calibrated to reflect and describe analytically the location of women of color in US culture" (222), then black feminists are challenged to reach deeply within ourselves and our communities and to use the tools at our disposal to create this necessary critical discourse.

III

In a particularly compelling section of "Variations of Negation," Wallace critiques Toni Morrison's novel *The Bluest Eye,* which Wallace states is about the collective internalization of self-hatred, the cultural erasure of a people, and the mostly unconscious battle with what Western civilization calls madness. The novel centers on the plight of Pecola Breedlove, who experiences physical and psychological abuse at the hands of her parents, Cholly and Pauline Breedlove. Pecola's parents internalize their rage and spew their collective self-hatred on their only child, slowly driving her insane. In the novel, Pecola's psychological devastation is sharply contrasted with the nurturing family experiences of Claudia, the young narrator of the story, and those of other black people in the community. By contrasting the positive identity and community life of Claudia and her sister with the cultural dysfunction, incest, and sordid family life of the Breedloves, Morrison metaphorically indicts Eurocentric cultural hegemony. Wallace contends that by portraying characters with the psychological resources to battle self-hatred, *The Bluest Eye* examines the strengths of black family and community as an antidote to "madness." But in a curious qualification for a writer enamored of rhetorical extremes, Wallace states: "I haven't done justice to the compositional complexity of *The Bluest Eye* if I've given the impression that this novel explicitly advocates black feminist creativity as a corrective for what ails the black community" (1990, 234).

Yet I believe precisely what seems too simple for Wallace to entertain. I would argue that creative acts out of a black feminist consciousness *can* correct what ails the black community. The intellectual contributions of black feminists are a vital part of the leadership needed to reclaim black communities as places of nurture and transcendence.

The issue of leadership in the black community raises the primary question that black and white Americans ask, namely, who's to blame for the problems of the black community? If we refuse, as we should, to blame our youth for the failures of community; if we refuse, as we should, to point fingers at idle, unemployed, hurting black men as the cause of black poverty and failed community; and if we refuse, as we should, to blame black women for conditions within the black community, then two further questions arise: Why should black women do anything for or about black communities? If we are not to blame for the plight of black communities in need, why should we care?

These questions arise because black women have been profoundly affected by the disconnection from their activist roots and by the negation of their role in the destiny of black people. Yet beyond alienation and negation lies another very practical question: What *can* black women do now? After all, we have already sacrificed much and suffered a great deal of abuse for the sake of our communitarian values. In many instances, we have endured communities that have taken us for granted, rejected our values, distorted our contributions, and squandered our assets while demanding that we bear our shame, ignorance, hurt, and poverty in mortal silence. Black women clearly understand that there are cultural tensions and critical issues to be addressed as blacks struggle to define themselves and their communities in light of today's social and political realities. It is also clear that entrusting charismatic leadership to a single group of individuals or to the elite of our race is as passé as the closely knit black communities that existed during legal segregation. But what do we have to replace the failed leadership and hurtful memories of our community's past? What, if anything, has feminism to say to black people as they struggle to identify new standards of leadership and new definitions of community?

Feminism has traditionally expanded the concept of community from one that denotes geographic location to one that denotes groups of people with self-defined characteristics. Although the black community has historically been a specific place or location, black people know that community is more than a phenomenon specific to place. For black people, community is a ritual presence that is not necessarily home or "hood." It is, however, being "at home." In its best sense, the black community embodies history and a feeling of connectedness with those who have similar traditions and a specific national, racial, and ethnic identity. Common characteristics of community include similar forms of cultural expression, religious or spiritual traditions, and kinship rituals. Community in this sense is a tie that binds individual blacks to a historical perspective on their ethnicity in relation to others who share similar group characteristics. When defined in this way, community is a pathway for black personal survival and social transformation.

Communities are networks and historical connections through which people learn the interplay between individual aspirations and shared group expectations. Although the social fabric, economic structure, or cultural norms of communities of place can destroy the humanity of the people who claim or are claimed by them, a sense of community is nevertheless essential to the survival of oppressed people. Thus, mobilizing ordinary black women to restore the liberating essence of community is an essential part of the next phase of the black struggle. Community building is more important to black women now than to any group of women in history. Black women need the collective fulfillment of traditional black communities, whether we actually live in them or not.

Acknowledging that black women need their communities is a necessary prelude to action. What really ails black people is their disconnection from positive communities that benefit from large numbers of active black women. In short, what ails the black community is the dormancy of its women. Wallace would probably agree that black women should reinvest in their traditions of community commitment, but I emphasize this particular of un-negation because it suggests that black women must play leadership roles in recreating the social, political, and economic fabric of black life. Questions of black feminist creativity, theorizing, and leadership therefore must affirm a commitment to nurturing the human spirit that is embodied in the best of community life.

Outside of community is madness. Outside of community is dysfunction. Outside of community is the domain of the Breedloves, humans without civilization. Affirming community is an antidote to alienation. For blacks, community is the obverse of a twisted slave legacy and of the great myth of white supremacy, both of which are woven throughout the fabric of Western civilization. Resistance against European cultural hegemony has always found leadership among black women, who have traditionally celebrated the rich complexities of human experience.

Given the current social and economic conditions of black people, black feminist creativity must address another legitimate concern Wallace raises: "My overall concern [is] with black feminist creativity in general and with the manner in which . . . media visibility may be allowed to substitute for female economic and political power" (215). High-profile black successes such as Michael Jordan and Oprah Winfrey have little to do with everyday black empowerment. How, then, can black feminist creativity translate into social, political, and economic power? How can this power be extended to black women, black men, and black children? The creativity of black people is a source of wealth that can be applied to expand our economic base, to create jobs for our people, to rebuild our neighborhoods, and to renew our spirits. Artists and intellectuals must again become warriors for art and for justice, and black communities must support their efforts to return home.

IV

The cultural production of black female writers is yet another particular of un-negation. The fictional universes of black women affirm our contributions to African American literary and intellectual traditions. Wallace's "Variations on

Negation" concedes the power of black writers to validate and to interpret African American culture. In fact, as part of another effort to explain her critique of black women writers and their role in perpetuating the myth of the superwoman, Wallace acknowledges the role of black women's writing in the creation of her own feminist consciousness: "Like many other black women of my generation, I eagerly awaited the publication or reissue of black women's books" (1990, 224). Although for Wallace, the role of black women writers in the making of a feminist tradition was a tremendous achievement, she doesn't hesitate to tell feminists that there is still so much more to do: "I felt rebuffed by the unwillingness of black women writers to deal with a contemporary urban context" (225).

Despite the controversy created by Wallace's *Black Macho and the Myth of the Superwoman* (1979) and her reflections about black macho and black feminism over the years, she is correct in asserting that black women's creative expressions should be broadly conceived and should explore many more dimensions of black women's experiences than they have done so far. Wallace is also correct in her contention that producing a creative act is not enough. Cultural production must be not only created but also properly used. This means that we black people must pay more attention to securing control of our cultural production to use it for our legitimate needs. The question of how we use the products of black creativity is important: "To compensate for ghettoization, black feminist creativity's concentration in music and now literature has become provocatively intense. And yet it is still difficult even for those who study this music and literature to apprehend black feminist creativity as a continuous and coherent discourse." (219). Why is our discourse broken and fragmented, as Wallace suggests? One obvious answer is that we are continually reacting to a fickle intellectual establishment that interrupts the organic development of black creativity. Another answer is that we are producing works that are about blacks but are written for a marketplace that finds only a relatively narrow set of our concerns to be of any interest. When black female creative writers place black women and black ways of knowing in the spaces between the black male hegemony of African American literature and the white male hegemony of the literary and intellectual establishment, their creativity manifests the power of black female discourse and affirms the teaching and healing powers of healthy black communities.

To the extent that black feminist creativity is a discourse connected to a nostalgic past or to a market economy that bears no resemblance to black needs and aspirations, our work is indeed fragmented and scattered. Many of our black artists and intellectuals, however, including black feminists, are exploring richer dimensions of human experience through the particular lens of being black. In their work, we see a rich discourse that explores more ethical ways to move human and institutional arrangements toward mutual respect and collective integrity.

This book is part of an ongoing process toward creating a continuous, coherent analytical and interpretive b(l)ackdrop for our celebration of womanhood and our rebuilding of community. It springs from the profound need for black women to create and sustain particulars of un-negation.

7. Feminist Leadership for the New Century

It is possible to evoke in people a genuine desire to transcend our more selfish interests and to respond to a larger vision that gives us a sense of purpose, direction, meaning and even community. Real political leadership provides that very thing; it offers to lead people where, in their best selves, they really want to go.

— **Jim Wallis,** *The Soul of Politics: A Practical and Prophetic Vision for Change*

I

Changing the face of today's feminisms will not be easy. It will require the leadership of women from all walks of life. It is not entirely clear that these leaders will come from the ranks of today's feminists. In the twenty-first century, feminist leadership will require women to be committed to finding common ground without resorting to shallow co-optation or false compromise. It will require women to combine personal transformation and public change. Feminist leadership will need to build strategic alliances based on mutual self-interest and ethical consensus rather than on political orthodoxy.

Reconciling diverse interests has often been a goal of feminist rhetoric, but successfully integrating gender, class, and coalition politics as a practical matter continues, more often than not, to elude us. On the national level, feminist activists often use strategies that strain their credibility with the constituency they claim to represent. For instance, many black women felt that when Congress reauthorized the Hyde Amendment in 1993, women's groups were too timid to point out that poor women's reproductive choices were inappropriately limited by the total ban on taxpayer-supported abortions. Although supporting federal subsidies for abortion under any circumstance, including the life and health of a poor woman, would have been highly controversial, a reproductive-rights agenda that excludes them from access to the reproductive choices enjoyed by the wealthy and the middle class is reprehensible. Yet few mainstream feminists took this position. This example suggests how difficult it is to organize women across class differences and still develop an ethical and coherent political agenda.

From a clear-eyed organizing perspective, mainstream feminism still lacks the skill and the diverse base needed to frame issues that a broad range of women can support. For example, liberal feminist activists favor child-support enforcement but often fail to connect the economic plight of women who have divorced deadbeat dads to the need for increased income support for working women whose ex-husbands' child-support payments are not enough to support their children. Millions of children live in poverty, but equity feminists often exclude issues such as job training, child care, welfare reform, adequate health care, affordable housing, equity in school financing, and juvenile justice from their equal-pay-for-equal-work agenda.

The passage of the Personal Responsibility and Work Opportunity Reconciliation Act of 1996 demonstrates how little influence feminists have on poverty policy in America. A recent study reports that 71 percent of recent welfare recipients with earnings in 1998 earned wages *below the poverty line.* In 1999, more than 9 million poor children lived in a working family. In short, significant poverty continues to exist while $54 billion over six years is being cut from the former entitlement system. Feminists should vigorously support changes in the current law. For example, the workforce participation rates that states are required to maintain should be reduced to eliminate harsh sanctioning policies and practices that have the effect of rationing needed services. Also, barriers to employment should be assessed, and the law should allow extensions of benefit time limits to ensure that a woman has adequate skills to obtain employment before her welfare benefits are cut.[1]

Few women are demanding a feminist politics that vigorously addresses poor women's concerns. White middle-class feminists have benefited from the feminist revolution, but they cannot sustain successful coalitions that include both working-class women and women with limited economic opportunities. Yet organizing women across class distinctions is critical to influencing state policy initiatives that are developing in the wake of the federal government's movement away from broad social-welfare policy.

State initiatives involve a host of human needs, including taxes, jobs, education, social welfare, housing, and economic development. These issues will not be affected by isolated racial groups or by women who are perceived as well-meaning but politically marginalized. Organized constituencies will need to come together to affect relatively conservative state and local legislatures, which listen most frequently to politically active and powerful segments of the electorate.

Although black feminists can take credit for keeping issues of poverty and race on the American political agenda during the self-indulgent 1980s, black feminist leaders in the 1990s became increasingly identified with the academy or the cultural elite, or with the concerns of international feminism, through which women in developing countries are mobilizing and creating a new grassroots movement. Although some black feminists continue to engage in issue organizing,[2] too few are involved in ongoing political action in local communities. Fewer still have organized successfully with poor and working-class women to protect their mutual interests. From an activist perspective, feminist politics is increasingly confined to organizing small groups of followers, whereas what is needed, especially for black women, is a strategy for large-scale mobilization.

The troubling lack of feminist leadership in general and black feminist leadership in particular is further complicated by poor PR. Most black women have no idea who black feminists are or what they stand for. As long as black feminists are marginalized and isolated, black women will remain fragmented and politically ineffective. Black feminist leadership, black advocates, and black activists need to develop and clearly communicate a vision for black communities and to initiate jointly a strategy for realizing that vision. The "vision thing" and its realization require black feminists to combat America's changing racial dynamic by coalescing with other ethnic groups. Unfortunately, the challenges of race and ethnicity are complicated by the travails of the black middle class. What political pundits once described as the "new black middle class" remains an enigma. Many are essentially not black (that is, they do not want to be defined in racial terms), not new (that is, they essentially have many of the same attitudes as affluent and politically conservative blacks of previous generations), and not, as it turns out, middle-class (that is, they do not have the same upward mobility as whites, and they are still harassed by institutional racism). These observations are not meant to scapegoat an expanding but still tenuous black middle class. They are meant to suggest that it is possible and necessary to connect the needs of poor and working-class blacks to the needs of repressed middle-class blacks who have trouble relating to their ethnic group but are interested in protecting their social and economic interests.

Although the explosive growth of the black middle class is a measure of black progress, blacks are increasingly sensitive to the decline of their communities and to the significant number of blacks mired in poverty. Moreover, despite their increasing numbers, middle-class blacks are aware that their overall wealth lags behind that of whites and that they are more susceptible to job loss generated by the application of new technologies, the opening of world markets, and calls for smaller government. Despite expanding opportunities in the new economy, many of the structural features of that economy potentially threaten the hard-won social and economic status of the black middle class. As they do the white working and white corporate managerial classes, government downsizing and the lean-and-mean strategies of major corporations threaten the black middle class.

The expansion of the black middle class also demonstrates the success of policies aimed at expanding economic opportunity. Middle-class blacks have succeeded in part because they have benefited from community support, individual initiative, affirmative action, and the War on Poverty. The black middle class has not taken full advantage, however, of the opportunities that attacks on affirmative action and black economic decline present. The fact that so many Americans, including blacks, are concerned about their economic security provides an opportunity for organizing and political action. Black women are particularly situated to exploit this opportunity. For example, they are increasingly grounded by personal experiences with corporate racism, institutional corruption, and the political neglect of the basic elements of a competitive labor market, namely, quality education, job training, urban reinvestment, and rural economic development. They are increasingly restive and concerned for the future of their children. They are, in short, ripe for organizing.

What are the feminist strategies for mobilizing women in this group? What outreach, education, and mobilization strategies are in place to increase the number of middle-class black women who become socially and politically active on behalf of black communities? How intentional and how successful have these efforts been both in mobilizing middle-class black women and in helping them to work with poor and working-class women to build coalitions across race, gender, and class? How many black women's organizations are pooling leadership and resources to mount national campaigns on behalf of black communities across America? Now is the time.

Leadership to promote black women's activism emanates from such groups as the Coalition of One Hundred Black Women, the National Council of Negro Women, the National Black Leadership Forum, Black Women in Sisterhood for Action, the National Political Congress of Black Women, the National Black Women's Health Project, the Rainbow Coalition, and countless local partnerships and initiatives in political action, economic development, education, housing, employment, and welfare reform. These efforts, though welcome, are not sufficiently focused on building multinational and multilateral coalitions or on initiating projects to help black women heal from sexual aggression, betrayal, and disillusionment. Healing and reconciliation are a prerequisite to rebuilding black women's political culture.

Four national events provide additional examples of the failure of feminist leadership: the nomination of Clarence Thomas to the Supreme Court, the Los Angeles uprising on the heels of the treatment of Rodney King, the murders of Nicole Brown Simpson and Ronald Goldman, and Michele Wallace's review of bell hooks's book *Art on My Mind.* I contend that feminist leaders could have used each of these situations as an opportunity to strengthen diverse strategic alliances. Yet in each case, the opportunity was missed, because each event and its aftermath exposed dilemmas that feminism will need to reconcile to remain relevant to social change.

II

On October 1, 1991, Clarence Thomas was confirmed as the 106th justice of the Supreme Court. The Bush nominee squeaked by the Senate with a vote of fifty-two to forty-eight, amid allegations of sexual harassment by then Oklahoma University law professor Anita Hill. In three days of riveting testimony, Hill charged Thomas with having made lewd and sexually graphic statements and advances toward her that were unwelcome and that, in her legal opinion, constituted sexual harassment. Sexual harassment, after all, was a crime, and it seemed reasonable that someone capable of such a crime should not become a member of our nation's highest court.

The Senate Judiciary Committee, filled with senators themselves tainted by allegations of corruption or sexual scandal—Orrin Hatch, Dennis DeConcini, Ted Kennedy, Strom Thurmond, and Howard Metzenbaum, among others—listened to Hill's convincing testimony and Thomas's equally convincing denials. To add to the outrage of mainstream feminists, it became apparent during the hearings that some members of the Senate staff had previously been aware of Hill's charges but had tried to prevent them from coming before the Judiciary Committee.

During the hearings, feminists provided network commentary and proclaimed that the shameful conduct of Thomas and the drama of the hearings were a "national teach-in" on the issue of sexual harassment. Under the circumstances, those senators who would go on to vote for Thomas were totally insensitive to the pain this crime caused its victims, most of whom were women. Those senators were targeted for political defeat by women's political organizations. Clarence Thomas won the nomination, but in 1992, Illinois democrat Carol Moseley-Braun became the first black woman elected to the Senate. She and a few other women politicians were immediate beneficiaries of women's political anger and disgust over the Anita Hill incident. (Moseley-Braun was defeated in her bid for a second term in 1998.) Many women realized while watching these hearings that the Senate was more of an all-male club than was good for the country. In retrospect, the Thomas-Hill situation helped elect a few women politicians and may well have enlightened some people about sexual harassment, but the episode obviously boiled down to who got the benefit of the doubt. That person certainly was not Anita Hill.

While Americans were coming to grips with the conflicting accounts of Thomas's behavior, the whole affair was raising old and hurtful political divisions in the black community. Black conservatives thought that Thomas's sex life should not deny us a black on the Supreme Court, whereas black academics, professional women, activists, and progressives, like me, felt that Thomas was George Bush's most cynical appointment. As such, he should have been rejected initially on his lack of qualifications and subsequently for his misogyny.

Beneath this overt political division was a strong gender tension that white feminists helped introduce with their overzealous embrace of Hill as a victim of sexual harassment. In their zeal to attack Thomas as an example of the sexual power that men can wield over women in the workplace, feminists inadvertently ignited gender flashpoints within the black community. As a result, many black women, using some form of perverse racial logic, chose to support Thomas. Those who chose to support Hill however bore the additional burden of having to distance themselves from white feminist agitators.

As the debate raged over Thomas's innocence or guilt, as well as over Hill's duplicity or complicity in the sordid affair, black Americans confronted other deep divisions between them. These were the painful divisions of gender, class, and the meaning of race. White feminists were so focused on sexual harassment that they didn't understand—didn't care to—that many black women were grappling with the very real concern that issues of gender and class were publicly compromising race solidarity. The Thomas-Hill affair suggested to the black community that race might never again serve as the basis for black social, political, or economic collective action.

Gender solidarity proved equally elusive. Too many working-class black women simply did not accept Hill as a victim. Sexual harassment is a daily occurrence in their lives, and to them Hill was not a victim of sexual harassment. She was a middle-class opportunist deluded by ambition and responsible for the poor choices she had made. Other women, including me, who conceded that her political ambition contributed to her ordeal felt that she still didn't deserve what she said had happened to her. Because racism is often still defined solely as denying black men the right of manhood, however, Thomas could position race and gender to his advantage. He did so, in this instance, by raising the question, what indignity that Hill had suffered was worth lynching him for? Despite a full-page *New York Times* ad, "In Defense of Our Name," signed by some 1,600 black women, and despite enough writing and commentary to produce one study of black women's views (Smitherman, 1995) and one well-received collection of essays on the subject (Morrison, 1992), the media found few pundits who would call into question Thomas's racial hocus-pocus. Of the high-profile mainstream feminists who commented on the hearing, none could infuse her sound bites with a strong and unequivocal feminist analysis of the race and class divisions that Thomas so neatly exploited for personal gain.

Paula Giddings published one of the most penetrating analyses of the Hill-Thomas affair. In her work, entitled "The Last Taboo" (1994), she advocated for open discussions of black sexuality, including the topic of the political and cultural effects of sexual aggression on black men and women. Unfortunately, not many black communities took this advice. Sadly, silence continues to surround the topics of sexual aggression and gender violence and their effects on the black community. This silence diminishes the black community's commitment to ending gender oppression.

III

The April 29, 1992, acquittal of four white Los Angeles police officers accused of police brutality in the beating of Rodney King, a black motorist arrested and charged with driving under the influence, resisting arrest, and disorderly conduct, was another missed opportunity for feminist leadership. The arrest was captured on videotape and showed that King was savagely beaten. The camera rolled as King fell to the ground and was repeatedly kicked by one officer as he lay prostrate. The tape seemed to capture clearly a black man being brutalized by the Los Angeles Police Department. Yet the physical evidence of police brutality, including the videotape, did not lead an all-white jury to find the police guilty.[3]

When officers Stacey Koon, Laurence Powell, Timothy E. Wind, and Ted Briseno were acquitted of having used excessive force, the verdict was widely perceived by the nation as a whole and by blacks in particular as a racist mockery of justice. Spontaneous rage sparked five days of insurrection in Los Angeles and brief but nasty skirmishes in other U.S. cities. Blacks were much more unified on the issues posed by King's ordeal than they were on the issues posed by Anita Hill's.

In South-Central Los Angeles, an overcrowded black and Latino neighborhood with an expanding Korean population and a legacy of entrenched inner-city poverty, the uprising was lethal. More than 50 people were killed, more than 2,000 people were injured, 3,000 people were arrested, 862 buildings were burned, and Los Angeles incurred more than $200 million in damage. During the violence, Reginald Denny, a white truck driver, was savagely beaten by three black youths, who were subsequently acquitted of the most serious charges.

President George Bush, in a nationally televised speech outlining plans to send federal troops to restore order, further incensed blacks by decrying the violence in Los Angeles as wanton lawlessness. Although Bush, who was running for reelection, announced a federal investigation to determine whether the police officers could be tried in federal court for violating King's civil rights, not once during his speech did he address the issues of police harassment, poverty, or racial tensions in South-Central, which many observers saw as the root cause of the violence.

President Bush's Justice Department subsequently filed a federal civil rights lawsuit on King's behalf. In 1993, officers Koon and Powell were convicted of violating King's rights. Despite this action, however, the president made no real effort to explore the complex racial, class, and immigrant substructure of the uprising. His lack of understanding beyond the typical law-and-order response was viewed as another of the president's cynical attempts to keep race and economic-justice issues off the national agenda.

Throughout this entire ordeal, mainstream feminists were relatively silent. Apparently, mainstream feminists do not see the brutality of anyone but women as a women's issue. As a result, they were unprepared to take up the cause of a black man who, whatever his faults, deserved justice. Feminist commentators also never mentioned Reginald Denny's forgiveness of his attackers or the common decency that exists between blacks and whites that was affirmed when black residents helped the unconscious truck driver and probably saved his life. Some activists were quick to criticize the Los Angeles jury that acquitted the youths charged in the beating (Gooding-Williams, 1993). Again the feminist response was muted.

The job of examining how U.S. domestic policy was responsible for the horror of South-Central fell to Maxine Waters, a congresswoman in whose district much of the violence occurred. Waters reminded President Bush and the nation that racial anger and economic deprivation breed urban violence. For a brief moment, the leadership of this black woman forced America to consider seriously the problems of urban poverty. Few prominent feminists joined Waters or the Congressional Black Caucus in their call for a federal indictment.

In the wake of the uprising, there was strong local organizing around jobs and economic development for America's cities. Judging by the responses received on Capitol Hill, feminist organizations didn't seem to support fully the campaigns for jobs for inner-city youths. Those few of us feminists who did, lost. The Summer Youth Employment Program, a prominent part of Clinton's economic-stimulus package, was defeated in the first ninety days of his presidency.

IV

The brutal murders of Nicole Brown Simpson and Ronald Goldman in June 1994 provided yet another missed opportunity for feminist leadership. O. J. Simpson, the American hero turned fallen icon, transfixed the nation in the bizarre aftermath of his stunning arrest. The Hall of Fame athlete, movie star, and media representative led the police on a nationally televised low-speed chase before being apprehended as the alleged killer of his ex-wife and her friend. The Los Angeles Police Department allegedly leaked information to expose the underside of Simpson's private life. The public was shocked to learn that Simpson had abused his wife and had pleaded no contest to a 1989 charge of domestic battery. This charge surfaced as a motive for the murders and was immediately seized upon by feminists as an opportunity to promote the issue of domestic violence.

Although domestic violence is a serious issue that deserves increased attention, feminists ignored the plight of black people who had lost Simpson as a hero because of relentless press attention, questionable police procedures, and a carnival of celebrity hype that was itself a travesty of justice. Moreover, mainstream feminists did not seem to realize that racism in the criminal-justice system is just as important to blacks as the horror of domestic violence. Once again, black women felt that they had to choose between their race and their gender when discussing this situation. When polls showed a substantial gap between blacks and whites over whether they thought Simpson could get a fair trial, the race issue surfaced and began to dominate every aspect of the trial, from the selection of the jury to the rendering of the verdict.

For mainstream feminists, the strategy of linking Simpson's past domestic abuse of his wife to the circumstantial evidence surrounding her murder provided both a criminal motive and a symbol for the tragedy of domestic violence. As feminists exploited this symbolism, they alienated black people, who had little reason to trust the Los Angeles Police Department or the Office of the Los Angeles County Prosecutor. Feminist commentators bashed Simpson as a wife beater turned murderer, yet few, if any, mentioned that a fair trial was an issue because the criminal-justice system punishes blacks more often and more severely than whites.

Mainstream feminists did not acknowledge the legitimacy of the black perspective, but they should have. After all, more than a half million black men are in American prisons. Moreover, the black community in Los Angeles had documented many instances of racism suffered by black men seeking justice from the Los Angeles police and courts. In short, racism mocks criminal justice in America, and everybody knows it, whether people want to admit it or not.

In their haste to exploit Simpson as a symbol of female victimization, feminists negated the deep and legitimate suspicion that the black community has of justice in America. They ignored the complexities of these issues and simply made Simpson an icon for domestic violence. When, as part of Simpson's defense, attorney Johnnie L. Cochran Jr. exposed key prosecution witness Officer Mark Fuhrman's racist attitudes, the testimony educated the entire nation about racial bias in the American criminal-justice system. Ultimately, the jury had no reasonable doubt about that. The racial divide exposed during the Simpson trial clearly demonstrated the limits of mainstream feminism. Other feminisms will not soon recover.

Simpson's acquittal in the 1995 criminal trial by a Los Angeles jury that included nine blacks was widely seen by whites as a mockery of justice. However, the verdict could be seen as an indictment of racism both in the criminal-justice system and within feminist orthodoxy. When a white jury in the subsequent civil trial convicted Simpson of battering Nicole Brown Simpson and causing the wrongful death of Ronald Goldman, Simpson was ordered to pay $33.5 million in compensatory and punitive damages. Mainstream feminists openly rejoiced but did not call for racial healing in the aftermath of the civil trial and made no effort to promote racial reconciliation. Moreover, lost in all of the media images of blacks cheering the criminal verdict and whites crying or standing in stunned silence were the complexities of the race and gender issues exposed during the trial. Lost, for example, were the voices of whites who believed Simpson was innocent and blacks who understood the racial divide but believed Simpson was guilty.

V

White feminists are not alone in their need for lessons in leadership. Michele Wallace's critique of bell hooks's *Art on My Mind: Visual Politics* (1995) is a case in point. This essay, "Art for Whose Sake?" (1995), criticizes everything about bell hooks but her shoe size. The most incredulous part of this vitriol is that Wallace essentially justifies her personal attack on hooks by saying it's a tough job but somebody has to do it. Hooks apparently needed to be punished for being a "one woman cottage industry," for "relentless guilt mongering," for producing her own work as cover art because it "imprints upon our consciousness [hooks's] humble working class origins in Hopkinsville, Kentucky," for earning a decent salary at City College of New York without teaching the number of classes that Wallace thought she should, and for her annoying practice of not using footnotes and appropriate documentation. Wallace claims that black feminists are terrified of hooks and that they do not attack her because "exposure of her excesses could call into question the intentions of all other black feminists and . . . the precious hard won academic appointments, anthologies, conferences, grants, and travel budgets as well."

Now, I really admire both hooks and Wallace, so this review bothered me. First, I wondered how much of it was prompted by Wallace's self-proclaimed role as black feminist critic of popular culture, art, and politics. In other words, how much of her critique is over turf and market share rather than hooks's intellectual effrontery? Second, how much of this critique is Wallace's reaction to the class distinctions between hooks's working-class intellectualism and Wallace's defense of the politically committed bourgeoisie? Third, and perhaps most important, I wondered how many readers simply dismissed Wallace's review as the ranting of a notoriously thin-skinned feminist instead of taking her criticism seriously. Although a one-sided tiff between two black academic feminist intellectuals is not comparable, for example, to the beating of Rodney King or the murders of Nicole Brown Simpson and Ronald Goldman, the principles at work in this spat are. Black women should take issue with each other whenever necessary, but they should not ground their criticisms in personal attacks.

Wallace does make excellent points about the shortcomings of *Art on My Mind.* For example, the struggles and sacrifices of black artists and art collaboratives that confronted race in the art establishment in the 1960s involved the Spiral Group, which hooks mentions, but also included Wesui, AfriCobra, the Kyumba Ya Sanaa Gallery in New York, and the Southside Community Arts Center and the Organization of Black American Culture (OBAC) in Chicago. Between 1966 and 1973, there were thirty major exhibitions of African American art in the United States (McElroy, Powell, and Patton, 1989, 73–115; *Black Art,* 1989). Like most readers of hooks's work, I wanted to know much more about these struggles from knowledgeable critics of the art scene. I'm less impressed, therefore, with Wallace's rottweiler-style attack on hooks, which takes up most of the article, than I am with Wallace's desire to interpret the relevance of the sixties protests in the arts community for today's black artists and art critics. If Wallace had spent more time on this aspect of her critique, I would be commending her as a paragon of black feminist leadership. But she didn't, so I'm not.

I never agree with everything Wallace or hooks says, but I don't want to be placed in the position of having to choose one of their voices over the other. I can only hope that Wallace writes the book that she criticizes hooks for not being able to pull off. Such a work would be a fascinating, satisfying, and concrete demonstration of black feminist leadership.

VI

As a new millennium begins, black feminism should focus on building an agenda whose goal is to improve the day-to-day lives of black women, their families, and their communities. Our main priority has to be rebuilding black communities and ending the crisis of black womanhood. But black feminists have a long way to go before theoretical insight engenders collective action. Gender identities are multiple and shifting, and the tensions between race and gender are easily ignited. So the journey ahead is undeniably treacherous, and victory is by no means assured.

Black feminist writing, organizing, and political action can help black women lift themselves to a new level of political consciousness. Black feminists cannot continue simply to write to each other from protected rooms and tenured positions in academe. The times demand that they hit the streets and work with the women there who are struggling against crime, drugs, teen pregnancy, welfare dependence, slum landlords, teen suicide, AIDS, environmental racism, child neglect, neighborhood disinvestment, prison conditions, and economic injustice. Working for our freedom will inform our theories better than refining our arguments in endless internal debates. To remain relevant to black people, black feminists must leave the communities to which they aspire and identify with the concerns of the communities they left behind.

Black women experience multiple brutalities because of gender, race, and class. They will respond to black feminist leadership if it moves them beyond anger and disappointment toward new forms of hope, solidarity, and transcendence. Beyond the collective rage and sense of betrayal, beyond the rejection of black men, and beneath the froth of our own unbelief, black women are beginning to recognize the impact of shifting realities — social, political, and psychological —

on those of us whom the rest of us would rather ignore. Such women neglect their children, abuse drugs, beat their elderly mothers, prostitute their bodies, get pregnant too soon and too often, or exploit their communities. They conjure up shame and silent hostility in part because, regardless of their class status, they are unstable, decentered, divorced from their history, and devoid of cultural knowledge. They are so minimal and minimized, so locked in self-pity, so trapped by feelings of worthlessness, so dependent on a consumer mentality, and so addicted to sexual gratification that they destroy themselves and their families. This destruction in turn eats away at the spirit of community and erodes the fabric of black political culture.

These women come from all backgrounds and exist in all social classes; they live among us. Often they are our friends, our daughters, our mothers, our coworkers, or our neighbors. In time, they become vacant and gaping hulks, often dressed up but rarely having anyplace to go except down. Too many of these women have sold their self-respect to the streets and are addicted to drugs, food, shopping, or soap operas. They have contorted their identities to deserve their degradation. They embrace their own victimization through self-righteousness, self-contempt, self-delusion, and self-destruction. To them, other black women have become cynical opportunists often dominated more by what is expedient than by what is right.

These black women are included in the nightly news more frequently than they are acknowledged in the production of black female intellectuals. Are these women beyond feminism, black or otherwise? If so, then what can be done for, with, and about them? If not, they require a feminism that insists on their self-worth, their power, and their responsibilities. They need a feminism that boldly accepts the challenge to help them heal themselves. These women and the feminists who reach out to them must reclaim a black female identity that ends their personal crisis and restores their sense of black womanhood.

As black feminists have confronted the overlapping contradictions of gender, class, and race, as well as the failed logic of traditional leadership, they have written far too little about the many black men who are at the mercy of a twisted patriarchy that imitates the master class. These men are exploited beyond recognition by street life and a cynical contempt for commitment. Street culture fascinates jobless young black men. Street life is the renegade spectacle whose images are exploited by an economy that creates narrow and degrading stereotypes of black manhood to entertain whites and politically unconscious blacks. The market success of these gargoyles of black masculinity all but ensures that future generations of black men will equate manhood with the capacity to make babies, the right to treat women like used commodities, and the right to intimidate people as a misguided expression of black rage.

These failures of black manhood and womanhood are often associated only with those locked in the dark labyrinth of urban ghettos. Yet the young inner-city black is but one horn of the black dilemma. We also have to contend with those members of the bourgeoisie who have little connection to or identification with the masses of black people. In fact, a growing number of beneficiaries of the civil rights struggle distance themselves either from politics or from their own ethnic past. They profess no cultural or community connection to black people and oppose progressive black political resistance. Black feminists should call for an immediate and ongoing dialogue with representative thinkers from these groups. In public forums, black people can fully explore the implications of different political perspectives on human sexuality. Our daughters and sons need to hear this conversation as they embrace their own racial and gender identities.

Despite disenchantment and confusion in the feminist ranks, despite mainstream concern over gender as a protected class, despite the need for new feminist paradigms, and despite the ever enduring popularity of *Cosmopolitan* magazine, this book proceeds from the premise that feminism is the only form of intellectual creativity whose specific aim is women's empowerment. Feminist theory presents multiple yet related frameworks of empowerment that can guide those of us who seek to rebuild social institutions and interpersonal relationships while engaging in struggles for social justice. For black people, these tasks require commitment to black cultural traditions and an insistence on a heightened gender consciousness in the service of progressive social change. The various strands of feminist theory are ineffective in dealing with the diversity of women's culture and in mobilizing a broad base of women and men unified around the human values inherent in feminist thought. The black feminist challenge is to confront issues of diversity, fairness, justice, and gender equity while reclaiming our historic standards of womanhood and rebuilding our communities. Reconstituting black feminisms as principled action can renew black women's political culture and can help America achieve its greater destiny.

8. Feminism, Black Women, and the Politics of Empowerment

There is no time to waste. Where poverty is growing among us, it must be initially contained and ultimately reversed. Where anarchy is growing among us, it must be initially contained and ultimately reversed. Where rabid materialism is growing among us, it must be initially contained and ultimately reversed. Where cynicism is growing among us, it must be initially contained and ultimately reversed. Where violence is growing among us, it must be initially contained and ultimately reversed. Where economic injustice is growing among us, it must be initially contained and ultimately reversed. Where racism and sexism are growing among us, they must be initially contained and ultimately reversed.

> —Sheila Radford-Hill, unpublished manuscript

Despite the fact that blacks remain socially and economically marginalized and a racial hierarchy is still intact in United States society, this community continues to have the capacity to alter radically the political landscape in favor of progressive social and economic policies.

> —James Jennings, *Race and Politics: New Challenges and Responses for Black Activism*

I

The value of feminist theory lies in its capacity to understand gender, the continuum of masculine and feminine behavior, as a social construct. Understanding the specific social and cultural relationships that sustain human sexuality empowers women to rewrite the history of human existence. Feminist theorizing engenders political consciousness and moves both men and women toward higher-order thinking about the meanings and opportunities inherent in sexual difference. Without feminist theorizing and its contentious politics, there would be little gender consciousness and less political activism on behalf of subjugated groups. In its slow and tortured way, the second wave of feminist agitation moved feminism closer to the possibility of an organic relationship between theory and social practice.

The promise of feminist theorizing cannot be realized, however, as long as issues of power, privilege, and race raise concerns about what aspects of women's experience are framed for discussion and by whom. The branches of second-wave feminism could not meaningfully articulate how or whether women's different but equally legitimate interests could be reconciled to issues of social justice, economic opportunity, and political parity.

To their credit, second-wave feminists stressed political action to change institutions, secure equal rights, enhance economic opportunity, and expand women's rights as sexual beings. Despite these accomplishments, second-wave feminism failed to predict or adequately explain the dilemmas and contradictions inherent in women's varied experiences. Divisive and sectarian debates, combined with the rise of social conservatism, produced a backlash against feminism. The critiques of feminist theory advanced in the late 1980s and early 1990s were written as an integral part of and in reaction to this attack.

The backlash within feminism continues to discredit the false idea of women as universal victims, the limiting political orthodoxy of feminist politics, and the failure of feminist theory strategically to reconcile social, cultural, and political differences among women. Prominent feminists have discarded the most objectionable aspects of the feminist revolution, like the bittersweet memories of a disappointing lover, in well-publicized disavowals and debates over questions of relevance, fairness, and diversity. Controversy turned feminism inward. Feminist theorizing became acutely aware of its limits and ambivalent regarding its role in fostering peace and justice. In time, the specialties and subdisciplines of academic feminism gradually became separated from the reality of most women's lives. This separation was, in part, an unintended consequence of winning the battle against the two most pernicious myths of Western feminism: the primacy of women's oppression and the essential nature of women.

The postmodern wave of feminist theory and research is dominated by microanalyses of women's experiences, often in the form of feminist critiques of long discredited social theorists or ideas. Beyond postmodernism, participatory feminist research embraces local solutions to social ills and documents the struggles of women who are active in their communities. In addition, ethnographic research, case studies, oral histories, and quantitative research document the struggles of women who are trying to heal from various abuses and addictions. Despite these changes in feminist research and discourse, feminist politics continues to alienate many black women and large segments of the black community.

Despite dwindling or distant support for progressive social change, black feminist theorizing challenges the broader feminist community to rethink the social categorizations of race, gender, and class. This discourse has been credited with confronting feminist theory and politics with a demand for the inclusion of diverse women's experiences. Notwithstanding this legacy, black feminism has missed opportunities to strengthen the connection between black women's gender identity and the quality of life in black communities.

During the second wave, black feminists focused on inclusion in the movement and all but ignored the rupture of gender identity caused by the attack of liberalism, feminism, black nationalism, and influential political leaders on black women's gender roles. As a result, black feminists demanded inclusion and equity for black women involved in the civil rights, feminist, and black power movements but failed to help them reverse the slow yet inexorable decline in their political culture and the attendant social decline in many of their communities. In the struggle for inclusion in the feminist movement, black feminist theorizing separated itself from the substance and processes of social change. This separation reinforced historical images of proud black womanhood but did not adequately connect these historic gender identities to the hard work of building black communities.

Since the 1960s, black feminist theorizing has failed to theorize adequately the consequences of the decline of black women's political culture. Because political activism is an integral part of building community and of passing cultural knowledge to the next generation, the move away from the roles of culture bearing and community building resulted in a decline of black women's empowerment. The crisis of black womanhood manifests itself through a loss of confidence in the power of collective action and through legitimate differences over whether and how black women can live politically conscious and committed lives.

An analysis of the social and economic status of black women as a group demonstrates why black women need to revitalize community activism. Because the future of our children and our communities is at stake, the success of any strategy for black progress has to be judged by how well it improves the daily lives of black people, especially poor women and their families. Ending the crisis of black womanhood will require black women to revive their political culture by building a social movement aimed at fostering progressive social change.

The movement to reclaim black womanhood and black communities needs to include educating new generations of black boys and girls about the historic standards of black womanhood. In addition, black women need to support each other in the process of healing from violence, sexual abuse, and various addictions. Finally, where appropriate, the new movement needs to include strategic analysis and political action across the divisions of race, class, and gender.

Energizing black women who are immobilized or unempowered is a vital part of the political socialization that is needed to rebuild a sense of community.

A black women's movement for progressive social change needs leaders who understand black women's ambivalence, anger, apathy, and feelings of powerlessness as well as their strength, resilience, and commitment to their families and communities. Embracing the need for black women's healing is just as important as revitalizing their social and political activism.

Recent analyses of feminist theory and its relationship to black leadership and black intellectuals correctly endorse radicalism as the approach most likely to benefit blacks and to hasten the demise of racial injustice. Over the last thirty years, feminist writers have extolled black leaders whose history includes a radical or uncompromising political stance focused on rapid and fundamental change in the social, economic, and political structure of American society. In conceding the power of black radicalism to quicken the pace of social change, writers should not ignore the shortcomings of radical politics. For example, because radicalism is positioned at the political extreme, it fosters dependence on social protest and charismatic leaders rather than on building the capacity of local organizations and national coalitions. Although black women have a proud legacy of radical political action, radical politics can also promote misogyny, homophobia, intolerance, and male domination of political and organizational decision making.

Feminists who privilege radicalism cite a legacy that black women need to reclaim, stretching from Sojourner Truth to Fannie Lou Hamer and Ella Baker (James, 1996, 47). But it was not just the radicalism of these leaders that made them noteworthy. Their most important contribution was their ability to get things done. It was their ability to mobilize and inspire large numbers of like-minded people to take action that was fundamental to the success of the movements they influenced and that made these women so valuable to the cause of black people. It was their ability to outmaneuver internal and external threats to the integrity of their movements that made them leaders. It was their ability to engage in consensus building rather than autocracy that made them great. The challenge of authentic feminist theorizing is to lay the foundation for the emergence of new leaders with the skills necessary to the task of building a contemporary political movement for social and economic justice.

The creative production of black women thinkers, writers, organizers, and leaders can help black women move collectively toward individual and collective empowerment. As it evolves, the new black women's movement will understand its past and dedicate itself to creating new forms of activism and education while engaging women from diverse groups. Future generations of black women's leadership will better negotiate the social contradictions and complexities that shape the cultural representations of women's experiences. Their work will mobilize black women and help them to redefine the power of gender and the strength of political action.

II

Renewing black women's activism is an idea whose time has come. It probably comes as no surprise, therefore, that on October 25, 1997, I joined the Million Woman March (MWM) in Philadelphia, Pennsylvania.[1] Flanked on one side by my cousin, who agreed to represent my parents' generation, and on the other side by my then twenty-one-year-old daughter, the City of Brotherly Love was resplendent with all the sisterly hues of the rainbow. Walking to Benjamin Franklin Parkway under overcast and threatening skies, my small family group harmonized with the pilgrimage. Police in the city estimated that 600,000 to 1 million women answered the organizers' call.

Phile Chionesu and the other Philadelphia organizers had planned the sequel to the October 16, 1995, Million Man March to attract all African American women regardless of socioeconomic status, sexual orientation, and religious or political affiliation. The event, the organizing activities, and the educational programs associated with the march were designed to celebrate and educate black women as well as to demonstrate the power of solidarity. The MWM was meant to engender black women's commitment to solve shared problems and to address mutual concerns. Judging from the attendance at the march as well as from the organizing that preceded and continued after the event, black women want their political legacy restored. After a generation of erasure, victimization, denigration, repression, and relentless attack, black women are reclaiming themselves.

The whole thing was amazing. Thousands of women came alone or brought their families. Thousands more came with church groups, union groups, professional organizations, sororities, or as part of grassroots organizing campaigns. Thousands came with only a few days' notice, and thousands more had been planning the trip for weeks. Hugs, welcomes, kisses, laughter, serious reflection, shopping, and just plain fun were bundled into the gathering of a dazzling array of black women. The MWM had some legitimate detractors, but black women welcomed the chance to be part of another historic moment in a long line of efforts to help "sistuhs" seek wisdom, solidarity, healing, recognition, and direction.[2]

Whether wearing the finest African attire or the disheveled look that said, "Wore this and rode a bus all night long to get here," the sisterhood was in force. Throughout the day, it was exciting to hear the words of black women like actress Jada Pinkett Smith, Congresswoman Maxine Waters, and rap artist Sister Souljah. Actor Blair Underwood promoted *Sisters, I'm Sorry,* an independent film about black male-female relationships. A number of local speakers echoed the meaning of the Million Woman March and its vision for black women. Restoration, repentance, and resurrection were themes of the march that were heard around the world. Each speaker explored these themes in the context of the need for black women to stand together across generations and despite differences. Dorothy Height spoke of our legacy of overcoming challenges and restoring community. She also talked about the significance of black women's leadership and proudly announced the opening of a national leadership center at the headquarters of the National Council of Negro Women. If it creates a pipeline for black women's leadership that is prepared to address issues of gender, family, and community, the Dorothy I. Height Leadership Institute will play a vital role in the reemergence of black women's empowerment. Later in the day, Winnie Madikizela-Mandela's speech connected black American women with worldwide liberation struggles.[3]

Before the march, women around the country had organized in small grassroots groups as part of their preparation for the march. MWM organizers worked with these groups to develop a platform. This platform was a national agenda for black women's political action. However, the political agenda unveiled at the march begs the question of how to revitalize black women's political culture at a time when many black women remain unconvinced of the power of collective action.

Although a specific focus for black women's activism is important, black women's ownership of any political agenda cannot happen without educating women who are politically uninvolved. In other words, black women require more than an agenda to crystallize political action. Their political culture must be revitalized in their hearts. Young black women need to understand how their mothers and grandmothers were practically stripped of a gender identity that incorporated a commitment to preserving their culture and building their communities. As black women accept the challenge of restoring black communities, they will need support to revitalize traditional gender roles that neither sacrifice individual needs nor replicate repressive gender relationships. If the ideals of the MWM are to succeed, organizers will need to address the underlying crisis of identity and crisis of belief that still exist among many black women. This will take all the outreach that came before the march, all that has come since, and all that is yet to come.

Developing and supporting public policy that addresses the needs, concerns, and aspirations of black women will increasingly require large-scale mobilization through networks of professional and grassroots organizations backed by sufficient authority to command political support. Black women will need policy-relevant social science and widespread political action around state and local policy initiatives affecting black gender interests. To wield national power will require strong engagement in party politics as well as strategic coalitions involving advocacy and public-interest groups.

Only time will tell whether having come together in the City of Brotherly Love will be acknowledged as the beginning of the resurrection of black women's political activism or another abortive effort that provides further evidence of the crisis of black womanhood. Whatever its ultimate significance, the march acknowledged black women's desire for grassroots activism on behalf of families and communities. Such activism is needed and will not be denied. The MWM made visible a critical mass of black women who are willing to work on behalf of themselves, their families, and the places where they live. In this way, the MWM demonstrated that black women are as eager as other women to work together to address shared concerns.

The march acknowledged the need for black women to find a new and more powerful connection to each other and to the struggle for justice and equality. As we move forward, black women will need leaders who are capable of building consensus and committed to helping them balance community building and culture bearing with progressive gender roles. These leaders will need to address the marginal economic status of black women as a group and to mobilize them to defeat misogyny and homophobia in society in general and in the black community in particular. They will need to operate from a vision of compassion, collaboration, and strategic consensus, rather than from a base of marginality, competition, and sectarianism. Black women's leadership can restore faith in collective action, heighten support for preserving our cultural heritage, and revitalize social and political institutions within the black community.

Nothing written in this book is meant to suggest that black men should not help or have not helped to build strong black communities. Nothing is meant to suggest that black men have not made tremendous contributions as leaders of the struggle for justice, equality, and democratic ideals. Their leadership will continue, as it should. Although the focus of this book is black female gender identity, my hope is that black male and female relationships will strengthen in an atmosphere that encourages political and cultural reflection on the role of gender, social consciousness, and black community in American culture and African American life.

III

The crisis in black women's identity and belief will end when every black woman has access to healing, solidarity, and political consciousness and when every black woman knows and accepts her share of responsibility to make all black communities places of nurture and transcendence for all black children. Although black women are far more complex and heterogeneous than any current theorizing would suggest, black feminists can work with local community activists to achieve this goal.

Many women resist describing themselves as feminists, but they still need to know the fallacies and the legacies of the women's revolution. In my view, black women can connect with a feminism that includes them and genuinely meets their needs. Feminists can document and influence the black community's connection to gender and political consciousness. Feminists can add what we have learned about women's struggles to create new forms of black social action. But this will require authentic feminisms. Authentic feminist theorizing engages in building relational and strategic frameworks to articulate the differences among women in terms of how gender consciousness is defined and used. Authentic feminisms acknowledge that a broad range of domestic and international quality-of-life concerns are women's issues. No feminism should promote gender politics that puts the narrowly defined interests of a social construct called "woman" ahead of the interests of real women and the values they uphold.

Standing together across generations and despite differences was a powerful subtext of the Million Woman March. The splintered and fragmented politics of the women's movement was nowhere to be found in the dampness of an autumn day in Philadelphia. From early morning to late afternoon, speaker after speaker exhorted us black women not to divide ourselves based on our differences. The speakers challenged us to explore the infinite opportunities to find common ground and to organize locally. Building on that base of strength, activists can mobilize women across class, gender, and race, when appropriate. In the new millennium, leadership committed to political action and armed with national strategies for rebuilding women's political culture is our best opportunity to rebuild our communities and our nation.

Epilogue
Suffer but Never Silently

Silence isn't golden when it comes to identifying and eliminating the crisis of black womanhood. I leave you with what I hope becomes part of your personal commitment to a politically active life.

Suffer but Never Silently

Suffer sometimes.
but never silently;
forget social approbation.
Say what you need; if you don't get it,
move on to someone who can/will give it to you.
Don't define yourself according to someone else's
feelings/needs/wants/desires;
focus on your own emotions and motivations.
Say what you can/can't do. Admit limits. Don't apologize.
Minimize your angst, not yourself.
Step into the light. Keep focused. Let all your demands
strengthen your resolve.

Notes

Preface

1. Sonia Sanchez captures the feelings that I am describing better than any other poet. See her *We a BaddDDD People* (1970), especially "blk rhetoric": "who's gonna make all that beautiful blk / rhetoric mean something" (15). See also Kazembe (1999), especially "james crow" (16–19).

Introduction

1. Notable exceptions include the pro-choice debates and the writings of black feminists such as Deborah K. King, Deborah E. McDowell, Hazel V. Carby, and Darlene Clark Hine, who tried in the 1980s to influence critical social debates in an era when intellectuals increasingly ignored the dynamics of race on the power relations in America and around the world. Throughout this period, young women grew increasingly alienated from politically correct feminism. See Rebecca Walker (1995, xxxv–xxxvi).

1. Toward an Authentic Feminsim

1. In her discussion of feminist identity politics, hooks states: "Often in these settings [where black women convene to talk about gender issues] the word 'feminism' is evoked in negative terms. . . . I hear black women academics laying claim to the term 'womanist' while rejecting 'feminist.' I do not think Alice Walker intended this term to deflect from feminist commitment, yet this is often how it is evoked. . . . [The term] is viewed as constituting something separate from feminist politics shaped by white women. For me, the term 'womanist' is not sufficiently linked to a tradition of radical political commitment to struggle and change" (1989, 181–82). See also Collins (1996).

2. Uses and Limits of Black Feminist Theory and the Decline of Black Women's Empowerment

1. Only a small part of Gordon's substantive arguments are presented here. Gordon's work explores the philosophical aspects of black existence using the insights of phenomenological existentialism. I explore critical race theory, but not primarily from a philosophical perspective.

2. In his essay "Race, Culture, Identity: Misunderstood Connections," K. Anthony Appiah provides an extensive historical critique of race, culture, and identity to argue

that there are no races (Appiah and Gutmann, 1996). Coauthor Amy Gutmann, in her response, entitled "Responding to Racial Injustice," argues that race discrimination is a fundamental principle used to perpetuate injustice in America. Society's benefits and burdens are unequally distributed on the basis of race. Gutmann argues that replacing unjust policies with just ones requires the use of color-conscious policies that are consistent with the fundamental equality of all human beings. She also argues for a change in the public debate based on the premise that a color-blind morality that is designed to be applied in an ideal society is not adequate to resolve the problem of color in our nonideal society: "Yet racial injustice in this society today is not simply derivative of economic, racial and educational injustice. Principles of economic and educational equity therefore are inadequate to resolve the problem of racial injustice. . . . When we take a close look at the claims of an ideal color blind morality applied without modification to our non-ideal society, we see much that is mistaken with such a simple application" (108).

3. Gender and Community

1. For a personalized discussion of issues related to middle-class and poor black children, see Marian Wright Edelman's *The Measure of Our Success* (1992).

2. Colin Greer, "Something Is Robbing Our Children of Their Future," *Chicago Tribune, Parade* magazine, March 5, 1995, 4–6. Greer cites interesting statistics regarding hunger in America at the time. Based on information provided by the Food Research and Action Center, more than 5 million children under twelve went hungry each month. Moreover, "42% of American children grow up in low-income families while of these, 23% grow up in households below poverty. This is double the child poverty rate of any industrialized country."

3. For a poignant discussion of this issue, see Haki Madhubuti (1990, 173–83).

4. For an example of this point, see Shelby Steele (1990, 93–109).

4. The Crisis of Black Womanhood

1. The history of black feminist organizing specifies the nature of the attacks against black feminists. Toni Cade Bambara describes the situation as follows: "We missed a moment in the early '60s. We missed two things. One, at a time when we were beginning to lay the foundation for a national black women's union and for a national strategy for organizing, we did not have enough heart nor a solid enough analysis that would equip us to respond in a positive and constructive way to the fear in the community from black men as well as others who said that women organizing as women is divisive. We did not respond to that in a courageous and principled way. We fell back. The other moment we missed was that we had an opportunity to hook up with Puerto Rican and Chicano women who shared not only a common condition but also I think a common vision about the future. . . . When people talked about multicultural or multiethnic organizing a lot of us translated that to mean white folks and backed off. I think that was an error" (1979, 238). In 1973, black women's organizing led to the formation of the National Black Feminist Or-

ganization (NBFO). Branches of the NBFO sprang up in more than ten cities, and more than four hundred women showed up for its first conference. By the end of the seventies, however, the organization had died (Schneir, 1994; Guy-Sheftall, 1995).

2. I thank Lawrence E. Grisham, whose remarks on October 31, 1997, to the Public Policy Session of the Futures Committee sponsored by the John D. and Catherine T. MacArthur Foundation and the Local Initiatives Support Corporation of Chicago (LISC) provided a sobering look at affordable housing. One of the source documents for his remarks was Jason DeParle, "Slamming the Door," *New York Times Magazine,* October 20, 1996, 52.

5. The Economic Context of Black Women's Activism

1. See also Masumura (1996). Masumura's report gives an idea of how the government defines poverty: "A poverty threshold is an amount of annual family income below which a family is deemed to be in poverty. Poverty thresholds vary by family size and composition and are updated each year to adjust for inflation. For instance, in 1994, the poverty threshold for a three-person family was $11,817" (2). In 1997, the poverty threshold for a family of four was $16,050, as reported by the U.S. Census Bureau.

2. See U.S. Bureau of Labor Statistics, *Mass Layoffs in November 1999,* February 2000, at http://stats.bls.gov/bls_news/archives/mmls_nr.htm (consulted March 27, 2000), especially table 1, "Mass Layoff Events and Initial Claimants for Unemployment Insurance, October 1999." See also National Governors' Association, *The New Economy: Governing in a Global and Technological Age,* December 1999, at http://www.nga.org/NewEconomy/Links.asp (consulted March 29, 2000).

3. Clinton E. Boutwell, "Profits without People," Phi Delta Kappa Educational Foundation, October 1997. See also "Top 20 Growth Occupations in Illinois," Illinois Occupational Information Coordinating Council, 1995.

4. For the trends in earnings of blacks, see Jaynes and Williams (1989, 276); U.S. Bureau of Labor Statistics, Labor Force Statistics from the Current Population Survey, *Unemployment Rate: Civilian Labor Force, Black Male, Age 16 Years and Older,* at http://stats.bls.gov/cpshome.htm (consulted March 29, 2000); U.S. Bureau of the Census, Current Population Surveys, *Poverty Status of People by Family Relationship, Race, and Hispanic Origin, 1959–1998,* March 1997, March 1998, March 1999, at http://www.census.gov/hhes/poverty/histpov/hstpov2.html (consulted March 29, 2000); and U.S. Bureau of the Census, Earnings by Occupation and Education, 1990, *Mean Annual Earnings in 1989 by Sex, Work Status, and Age* (using Race: Black, not of Hispanic Origin and Sex: Male and Female), at http://www.census.gov/hhes/www/income/html (consulted March 29, 2000).

5. *The Personal Responsibility and Work Opportunity Reconciliation Act of 1996 (PL 104–193) Short Summary,* National Governors' Association, September 16, 1996.

6. In 1999, the Urban Institute published a series of studies on aspects of welfare reform. One study analyzed how women who left welfare shortly after the enactment of the Personal Responsibility and Work Opportunity Reconciliation Act of 1996 were doing

one year after leaving welfare. Pamela Loprest (1999) reports the following key findings. Most women leaving welfare in 1997 were working in low-wage jobs and struggling to balance their work schedules with child care. One-third of former welfare recipients reported concerns about having enough food to feed their families each month. More than 38 percent reported having trouble paying rent or a mortgage. Nearly 30 percent reported having returned to welfare within the year. Twenty percent reported that they had not returned to welfare but were not employed (1–4).

7. For the statistics cited in each area of analysis, see the following sources by the U.S. Bureau of the Census (all at http://www.census.gov, consulted March 24, 2000): *Selected Economic Characteristics of Persons and Families by Sex and Race,* March 1997; *Selected Characteristics of the Population below the Poverty Level in 1998,* July 1998; *Selected Social Characteristics of the Population by Sex, Region, and Race,* July 1998; *Total Money Income in 1996 of Persons Twenty-Five Years Old and Over by Education, Region, and Race,* July 1998; *Poverty Status of People by Family Relationship, Race, and Hispanic Origin, 1959–1998,* March 1999; and *Population Estimates of the United States by Sex, Race, and Hispanic Origin, April 1990 to November 1, 1999,* December 23, 1999. See also U.S. Bureau of Labor Statistics, *Mass Layoffs in November 1999,* February 2000, at http://stats.bls.gov/bls_news/archives/mmls_nr.htm (consulted March 24, 2000); Dalaker and Naifeh (1998); National Governors' Association, *The New Economy: Governing in a Global and Technological Age,* December 1999, at http://www.nga.org/NewEconomy/ Links.asp (consulted March 29, 2000), and *105th Congress—Legislative Issues Wrap-Up,* at http://www.nga.org/105Congress/Index.htm (consulted January 21, 2000); and U.S. Centers for Disease Control and Prevention, *HIV/AIDS Surveillance Supplemental Report,* 1998 midyear ed., September 1999.

8. For an insightful discussion of the erosion of the middle class, see Donald L. Barlett and James B. Steele (1992, 1–31).

9. See National Governors' Association, *105th Congress—Legislative Issues Wrap-Up,* at http://www.nga.org/105Congress/Index.htm (consulted January 21, 2000).

6. The Particulars of Un-Negation

1. See Gates (1990, 52–68) and Wallace (1990, 213–43). All references to "Variations on Negation and the Heresy of Black Feminist Creativity" refer to the latter version of the work. Page numbers are cited parenthetically within the text.

2. Another fascinating aspect of dark matter, black holes, and the universe is that some astronomers now believe that there are black holes at the center of galaxies, including the Milky Way.

7. Feminist Leadership for the New Century

1. For more information on these issues, see *Welfare to What? Early Findings on Family Hardship and Well-Being,* Children's Defense Fund and the National Coalition for the Homeless, 1998.

2. Noteworthy examples include Angela Davis's conferences on prisoners and prison conditions, as well as her ongoing organizing in Oakland, California. In addition, the feminist contingent at the Black Radical Congress, held in Chicago in 1998, made its presence felt and heard in the action agenda that came out of the conference.

3. In *Official Negligence: How Rodney King and the Riots Changed Los Angeles and the LAPD* (1997), Lou Cannon makes several important points regarding the videotape of the Rodney King beating, which was shot by George Holliday from his balcony. A three-second segment of the tape was excluded from what was shown on network television; however, this segment was shown to the Simi Valley jury. This part of the tape showed King charging Officer Laurence Powell. Cannon asserts that the jury saw a videotape different from the one seen by the general public, a tape showing a black man with a weight lifter's physique repeatedly resisting arrest. Moreover, Cannon asserts that the destruction wrought in the subsequent uprising was due to official negligence by the Los Angeles Police Department and Chief Daryl Gates, who for various reasons delayed orders to South-Central command. This delay in the early stages of the uprising allowed it to develop sufficient momentum to proceed unchecked once the orders did arrive from Central command. Finally, Cannon, having investigated police practices and city policies, concludes that the King beating was the result of a flawed policy endorsed by the mayor and the city council. In Cannon's view, the beating was not just another incidence of police brutality.

8. Feminism, Black Women, and the Politics of Empowerment

1. An earlier draft of this book was criticized for focusing on the Million Woman March (MWM) and not including a broader range of black women's organizing efforts. The focus on the Million Woman March stems from my participation in the event, not from any desire to exclude any radical or progressive women's organizing.

2. Although the focus of this chapter is on the positive aspects of the MWM, there were a number of political and social challenges associated with the march that were evident throughout the day. These challenges included speakers who canceled their appearances, hoping their absence would make a political statement about the march, its organizers, and the other speakers who participated. Additional problems ranged from poor sound equipment to disagreements among participants about the behavior of women who were attracted to the commercial or social rather than the spiritual or political aspects of the march. Although these problems were disturbing, they should be viewed in the context of the work that was accomplished.

3. The invitation extended to Winnie Madikizela-Mandela was the most controversial aspect of the Million Woman March. At the time of the march, Madikizela-Mandela had been summoned before the South African Truth and Reconciliation Commission to explain her role in gross human-rights violations, including abduction, assault, and murder in connection with the activities of her United Football Club. In local meetings to organize participation in the MWM, the invitation to Madikizela-Mandela was discussed. Al-

though many women disagreed with the decision to invite her, they continued to support the march. Others boycotted the event. In South Africa, the grassroots popularity of Madikizela-Mandela was evidenced by the fact that in 1997 she was almost nominated as a candidate for deputy president of the African National Congress.

Selected Bibliography

Appiah, K. Anthony, and Amy Gutmann. 1996. *Color Conscious: The Political Morality of Race.* Princeton: Princeton University Press.

Archer, Margaret S. 1988. *Culture and Agency: The Place of Culture in Social Theory.* Cambridge: Cambridge University Press.

Baker, Houston A. 1984. *Blues, Ideology, and Afro-American Literature: A Vernacular Theory.* Chicago: University of Chicago Press.

Bambara, Toni Cade. 1979. "Commitment: Toni Cade Bambara Speaks." In *Sturdy Black Bridges: Visions of Black Women in Literature,* edited by Roseann P. Bell, Bettye J. Parker, and Beverly Guy-Sheftall. New York: Anchor.

———. ed. 1970. *The Black Woman: An Anthology.* New York: New American Library.

Barlett, Donald L., and James B. Steele. 1992. *America: What Went Wrong?* Kansas City: Andrews & McMeel.

Barrett, Michèle, and Anne Phillips, eds. 1992. *Destabilizing Theory: Contemporary Feminist Debates.* Stanford: Stanford University Press.

Beauvoir, Simone de. [1953] 1974. *The Second Sex.* Translated by H. M. Parshley. New York: Vintage.

Bell, Roseann P., Bettye J. Parker, and Beverly Guy-Sheftall, eds. 1979. *Sturdy Black Bridges: Visions of Black Women in Literature.* New York: Anchor.

Black Art/Ancestral Legacy: The African Impulse in African-American Art. 1989. Dallas: Dallas Museum of Art.

Bonner, Marita. [1925] 1991. "On Being Young — A Woman — and Colored." In *Bearing Witness: Selections from African-American Autobiography in the Twentieth Century,* edited by Henry Louis Gates Jr. New York: Pantheon.

Brown, Helen Gurley. 1982. *Having It All: Love, Success, Sex, Money...Even If You're Starting with Nothing.* New York: Pocket Books.

Cannon, Lou. 1997. *Official Negligence: How Rodney King and the Riots Changed Los Angeles and the LAPD.* New York: Times Books.

Churchill, Ward, and Jim Vander Wall. 1990. *The COINTELPRO Papers: Documents from the FBI's Secret Wars against Domestic Dissent.* Boston: South End.

Clough, Patricia Ticineto. 1994. *Feminist Thought: Desire, Power, and Academic Discourse.* Oxford: Blackwell.

Collins, Patricia Hill. 1991. *Black Feminist Thought: Knowledge, Consciousness, and the Politics of Empowerment.* New York: Routledge.

———. 1996. "What's in a Name? Womanism, Black Feminism, and Beyond." *Black Scholar* 26, no. 1 (winter–spring): 9–17.

———. 1998. *Fighting Words: Black Women and the Search for Justice.* Minnesota: University of Minnesota Press.

Cooper, Anna Julia. 1892. *A Voice from the South: By a Black Woman of the South.* Xenia, Ohio: Aldine.

Dalaker, Joseph, and Mary Naifeh. 1998. *Poverty in the United States, 1997.* Current Population Reports. Washington: U.S. Bureau of the Census. September.

Davies, Carole Boyce. 1994. *Black Women, Writing, and Identity: Migrations of the Subject.* New York: Routledge.

Davis, Angela Y. 1973. "Reflections on the Black Woman's Role in the Community of Slaves." In *Contemporary Black Thought,* edited by Robert Chrisman and Nathan Hare. Indianapolis: Bobbs-Merrill.

———. 1981. *Women, Race, and Class.* New York: Vintage.

de Lauretis, Teresa, ed. 1986. *Feminist Studies, Critical Studies.* Bloomington: Indiana University Press.

Denby, Charles [Matthew Ward]. 1989. *Indignant Heart: A Black Worker's Journal.* Wayne State University Press.

Dunayevskaya, Raya. 1996. *Women's Liberation and the Dialectics of Revolution: Reaching for the Future.* Detroit: Wayne State University Press.

Edelman, Marian Wright. 1987. *Families in Peril: An Agenda for Social Change.* Cambridge: Harvard University Press.

———. 1992. *The Measure of Our Success: A Letter to My Children and Yours.* Boston: Beacon.

Faludi, Susan. 1992. *Backlash: The Undeclared War against American Women.* New York: Anchor.

Fox-Genovese, Elizabeth. 1991. *Feminism without Illusions: A Critique of Individualism.* Chapel Hill: University of North Carolina Press.

Freire, Paulo. 1985. *The Politics of Education: Culture, Power, and Liberation.* Translated by Donaldo Macedo. South Hadley, Mass.: Bergin & Garvey.

Gardner, Howard. 1993. "Seven Creators of the Modern Era." In *Creativity,* edited by John Brockman. New York: Simon & Schuster.

Gatens, Moira. 1992. "Power, Bodies, and Difference." In *Destabilizing Theory: Contemporary Feminist Debates,* edited by Michèle Barrett and Anne Phillips. Stanford: Stanford University Press.

Gates, Henry Louis, Jr., ed. 1990. *Reading Black, Reading Feminist: A Critical Anthology.* New York: Meridian.

Gates, Henry Louis, Jr., and Cornel West. 1997. *The Future of the Race.* New York: Vintage.

Giddings, Paula. 1984. *When and Where I Enter: The Impact of Black Women on Race and Sex in America.* New York: Morrow.

———. 1994. "The Last Taboo." In *Unequal Sisters: A Multicultural Reader in U.S. Women's History,* edited by Vicki L. Ruiz and Ellen Carol DuBois. 2d ed. New York: Routledge. First published in *Race-ing Justice, En-gendering Power: Essays on Anita Hill, Clarence Thomas, and the Construction of Social Reality,* edited by Toni Morrison. New York: Pantheon, 1992.

Goldberg. David Theo, ed. 1990. *Anatomy of Racism.* Minneapolis: University of Minnesota Press.

Gooding-Williams, Robert, ed. 1993. *Reading Rodney King/Reading Urban Uprising.* New York: Routledge.

Gordon, Lewis R., ed. 1997. *Existence in Black: An Anthology of Black Existential Philosophy.* New York: Routledge.

Gottfried, Heidi, ed. 1996. *Feminism and Social Change: Bridging Theory and Practice.* Urbana: University of Illinois Press.

Guy-Sheftall, Beverly, ed. 1995. *Words of Fire: An Anthology of African-American Feminist Thought.* New York: New Press.

Harrison, Bennett. 1994. *Lean and Mean: The Changing Landscape of Corporate Power in the Age of Flexibility.* New York: Basic.

Hartsock, Nancy. 1996. "Theoretical Bases for Coalition Building: An Assessment of Postmodernism." In *Feminism and Social Change: Bridging Theory and Practice,* edited by Heidi Gottfried. Urbana: University of Illinois Press.

Heilbroner, Robert, and Lester Thurow. 1994. *Economics Explained: Everything You Need to Know about How the Economy Works and Where It's Going.* Rev. ed. New York: Simon & Schuster.

Herrnstein, Richard J., and Charles Murray. 1994. *The Bell Curve: Intelligence and Class Structure in American Life.* New York: Free Press.

Hine, Darlene Clark, and Kathleen Thompson. 1998. *A Shining Thread of Hope.* New York: Broadway.

hooks, bell. 1981. *Ain't I a Woman: Black Women and Feminism.* Boston: South End.

———. 1984. *Feminist Theory from Margin to Center.* Boston: South End.

———. 1989. *Talking Back: Thinking Feminist, Thinking Black.* Boston: South End.

———. 1995. *Art on My Mind: Visual Politics.* New York: New Press.

Huntington, Patricia. 1997. "Fragmentation, Race, and Gender: Building Solidarity in the Postmodern Era." In *Existence in Black: An Anthology of Black Existential Philosophy,* edited by Lewis R. Gordon. New York: Routledge.

James, Joy. 1996. *Transcending the Talented Tenth: Black Leaders and American Intellectuals.* New York: Routledge.

James, Stanlie M., and Abena P. A. Busia, eds. 1993. *Theorizing Black Feminisms: The Visionary Pragmatism of Black Women.* London: Routledge.

Jaynes, Gerald David, and Robin M. Williams Jr., eds. 1989. *A Common Destiny: Blacks and American Society,* by the Committee on the Status of Black Americans, Commission on Behavioral and Social Sciences and Education, National Research Council. Washington: National Academy Press.

Jennings, James, ed. 1997. *Race and Politics: New Challenges and Responses for Black Activism.* London: Verso.

Jones, Landon Y. 1980. *Great Expectations: America and the Baby Boom Generation.* New York: Ballantine.

Kazembe, Lasana. 1999. *Nappyheaded Blackgirls.* Chicago: IBIS Communications.

King, Deborah K. 1988. "Multiple Jeopardy, Multiple Consciousness: The Context of a Black Feminist Ideology." *Signs* 14, no. 1 (autumn):42–72.

Liu, Tessie. 1994. "Teaching Differences among Women from a Historical Perspective: Rethinking Race and Gender as Social Categories." In *Unequal Sisters: A Multicultural Reader in U.S. Women's History,* edited by Vicki L. Ruiz and Ellen Carol DuBois. 2d ed. New York: Routledge.

Locke, Alain, ed. [1925] 1977. *The New Negro.* New York: Atheneum.

Loprest, Pamela. 1999. *How Families That Left Welfare Are Doing: A National Picture.* Washington: Urban Institute. http://www.urbaninstitute.org/authors/loprest.html

Madhubuti, Haki R. 1990. *Black Men: Obsolete, Single, Dangerous? Afrikan American Families in Transition: Essays in Discovery, Solution, and Hope.* Chicago: Third World.

Martin, Joanne M., and Elmer P. Martin. 1985. *The Helping Tradition in the Black Family and Community.* Silver Spring, Md.: National Association of Social Workers.

Masumura, Wilfred T. 1996. *Dynamics of Economic Well-Being: Income, 1992 to 1993: Moving up and down the Income Ladder.* Current Population Reports. Washington: U.S. Bureau of the Census. June. http://www.census.gov.hhes/www/income.html (available March 29, 2000).

McDougald, Elsie Johnson. [1925] 1977. "The Task of Negro Womanhood." In *The New Negro,* edited by Alain Locke. New York: Atheneum.

McElroy, Guy C., Richard J. Powell, and Sharon F. Patton. 1989. *African-American Artists, 1880–1987: Selections from the Evans-Tibbs Collection.* Washington: Smithsonian Institution Traveling Exhibition Service, in association with University of Washington Press, Seattle.

Mishel, Lawrence, and Jared Bernstein. 1994. *The State of Working America.* Washington: Economic Policy Institute.

Morrison, Toni, ed. 1992. *Race-ing, Justice, En-gendering Power: Essays on Anita Hill, Clarence Thomas, and the Construction of Social Reality.* New York: Pantheon.

[Moynihan, Daniel P.]. 1965. *The Negro Family: The Case for National Action.* Washington: U.S. Department of Labor, Office of Policy Planning and Research.

Murray, Charles A. 1984. *Losing Ground: American Social Policy, 1950–1980.* New York: Basic.

Naples, Nancy, A., ed. 1998. *Community Activism and Feminist Politics: Organizing across Race, Class, and Gender.* New York: Routledge.

National Urban League. 1998. *The State of Black America.* New York: National Urban League.

New York City Commission on Human Rights. 1972. *Women's Role in Contemporary Society: The Report of the New York City Commission on Human Rights, Sept. 21–25, 1970.* New York: Avon.

Oakley, Ann. 1997. "A Brief History of Gender." In *Who's Afraid of Feminism? Seeing through the Backlash,* edited by Ann Oakley and Juliet Mitchell. New York: New Press.

Outlaw, Lucius T. 1990. "Toward a Critical Theory of Race." In *Anatomy of Racism,* edited by David Theo Goldberg. Minneapolis: University of Minnesota Press.

Pelto, Pertti J. 1970. *Anthropological Research: The Structure of Inquiry.* New York: Harper & Row.

Phillips, Kevin. 1990. *The Politics of Rich and Poor: Wealth and the American Electorate in the Reagan Aftermath.* New York: Random House.

Radford-Hill, Sheila. 1986. "Feminism as a Model for Social Change." In *Feminist Studies, Critical Studies,* edited by Teresa de Lauretis. Bloomington: Indiana University Press.

Reich, Robert B. 1991. *The Work of Nations: Preparing Ourselves for Twenty-First-Century Capitalism.* New York: Knopf.

Sanchez, Sonia. 1970. *We a BaddDDD People.* Detroit: Broadside.

Schneir, Miriam. 1994. *Feminism in Our Time: The Essential Writings, World War II to the Present.* New York: Vintage.

Scott, Kesho Yvonne. 1991. *The Habit of Surviving: Black Women's Strategies for Life.* New Brunswick, N.J.: Rutgers University Press.

Sharpley-Whiting, T. Denean. 1998. *Frantz Fanon: Conflicts and Feminisms.* Lanham, Md.: Rowman & Littlefield.

Smitherman, Geneva, ed. 1995. *African-American Women Speak Out on Anita Hill–Clarence Thomas.* Detroit: Wayne State University Press.

Sommers, Christina Hoff. 1994. *Who Stole Feminism? How Women Have Betrayed Women.* New York: Simon & Schuster.

Sowell, Thomas. 1994. *Race and Culture: A World View.* New York: Basic Books.

Spillers, Hortense. 1984. "Interstices: A Small Drama of Words." In *Pleasure and Danger: Exploring Female Sexuality,* edited by Carole S. Vance. Boston: Routledge & Kegan Paul.

Steele, Shelby. 1990. *The Content of Our Character: A New Vision of Race in America.* New York: St. Martin's.

Thompson, Sharon. 1984. "Search for Tomorrow: On Feminism and the Reconstruction of Teen Romance." In *Pleasure and Danger: Exploring Female Sexuality,* edited by Carole S. Vance. Boston: Routledge & Kegan Paul.

Walker, Alice. 1984. *In Search of Our Mothers' Gardens: Womanist Prose.* San Diego: Harvest–Harcourt Brace Jovanovich.

———. 1996. *The Same River Twice: Honoring the Difficult.* New York: Washington Square.

Walker, Rebecca, ed. 1995. *To be real: Telling the Truth and Changing the Face of Feminism.* New York: Anchor.

Wallace, Michele. 1979. *Black Macho and the Myth of the Superwoman.* New York: Dial.

———. 1990. *Invisibility Blues: From Pop to Theory.* London: Verso.

———. 1995. "Art for Whose Sake?" *Women's Review of Books,* October, 8.

Wilson, William Julius. 1987. *The Truly Disadvantaged: The Inner City, the Underclass, and Public Policy.* Chicago: University of Chicago Press.

———. 1996. *When Work Disappears: The World of the New Urban Poor.* New York: Knopf.

Yuval-Davis, Nira. 1997. "Women, Ethnicity, and Empowerment." In *Who's Afraid of Feminism? Seeing through the Backlash,* edited by Ann Oakley and Juliet Mitchell. New York: New Press.

Zack, Naomi. 1997. "Race, Life, Death, Identity, Tragedy, and Good Faith." In *Existence in Black: An Anthology of Black Existential Philosophy,* edited by Lewis R. Gordon. New York: Routledge.

Index

Created by Eileen Quam

117

Sheila Radford-Hill is an independent scholar with more than twenty-five years of experience in education, educational administration, advocacy, and policy development. She currently serves as division administrator for the Illinois State Board of Education, where she supports statewide policy initiatives and manages grant programs. She has lectured and written numerous articles and reports on education and advocacy issues.